More Joy More Genius

Humanizing K-12 For Deeper Learning

Don Berg

Don Berg

Photos on pp. 79, 166

By Richard Sloan

Illustrations on pp. 90, 103-106

By Eliana Bastidas

CONTENTS

Don Berg

INTRODUCTION: BACK TO BASICS?

I first began to sense the wrongness in elementary school. I got the first articulation of it from my friend Clark Jett as we were lining up at the end of recess one day in sixth grade. Clark and I were enrolled in a public magnet program for smart (but not quite "Talented and Gifted") students at Signal Hill Elementary School in Long Beach, California. It was 1978 or 79 and we were bussed in from Lakewood, a mostly white neighboring city. That particular form of "desegregation" meant that we had only two daily chances to meet the "regular" (meaning mostly black) kids: before school, *if* our busses got there early, and at lunch time. The rest of the time we were in separate classrooms from them (there was only one black kid in the program and he came by bus, too). There were occasionally some violent playground conflicts between us and them, though not serious enough to report it to the adults, as I recall. At the end of that recess Clark had pointed out that we were bussed in because we were pawns in an adult game. That observation was my first anchor for understanding the vague sense of wrongness that I had. I have since realized that the political game of adults was not really the problem, but was a symptom of the deeper problem that led to us perceiving ourselves as pawns controlled by people we didn't know or trust.

That same year my Mom asked me what I wanted to be when I grew up. I replied that I wanted to be a professional student. That was because I love learning. It was not because I had any particular liking for school. School was just something that I had to put up with; had I liked school

I would probably have envisioned myself as a teacher. For me learning was always much bigger and better than school.

Despite my negative attitude towards school, I was fortunate to be offered the opportunity to attend three different magnet programs. I accepted the offers to attend the SHARP program[1] at Signal Hill for fifth and sixth grades and PACE at Long Beach Polytechnic High School for tenth through twelfth grades. I declined the offer to join the TAG program during Junior High. As I recall, my choice to attend a regular junior high school was informed by some resistance to the bussing and the sense of being a pawn. The decision to attend the PACE program was informed by my boredom in the regular program and how my brother Jim, who had just graduated from high school, put college on my radar. PACE, the Program for Accelerated Curricular Experience,[2] was all about college preparation, so I put up with the daily commute to a predominantly black school[3] for another few years so I could ride the rails of being college-bound.

Despite gaining obvious advantages from the school system, I still knew intuitively that there was a wrongness there. Clark's insight about our being pawns never left me. Despite identifying as an enthusiastic learner I was stressed out by the demands of school. In high school I developed a variety of symptoms of stress: insomnia, constipation, hemorrhoids, etc. At the same time I was cursed with "potential." My teachers lamented that I was plenty smart enough to do the work but, mysteriously, I didn't have enough motivation to be conscientious about completing it. I didn't get very good grades, relative to the standards set

---

[1] I don't recall what the acronym stood for. It no longer exists.

[2] The 'A' now stands for "Additional," but I'm pretty sure it was "Accelerated" when I was there. The PACE program also had more black students, made more efforts to overcome racism, and still exists.

[3] If you detect a hint of racism, you are correct. One of the ways that I dealt with my vague sense of the wrongness and the few incidents of violence during that time was to categorically blame black people; this was consistent with the attitudes of a few other people around me. It was not an attitude that lasted, but it was part of my childhood experience. My high school diploma is from Lakewood High School because I took the option of attending the PACE program at Poly in the morning with a lunchtime commute to Lakewood for the afternoon. Most of my social life was determined by the sports I played for Lakewood.

by my college-bound peers. Later in chapter 1 I share the story of how I substantially improved my SAT score through fauxchievement, the pattern of fake learning that is pervasive throughout our school system. Fauxchievement is when you go through the motions without mastering the material. Everyone I've ever talked to who was successful in school used it at one time or another, often regularly. I  was able to game the system to get into an elite college, but in the process my enjoyment of academic learning was decimated. For example, after leaving college in 1989 it took over two years for me to read for pleasure again.

I had accepted and played out my role as a pawn in the public school system in exchange for getting into Reed College. Unfortunately, I was so motivationally damaged that I dropped out after three years. I then redirected my adult life to address the problems in K-12[4] education. I finally completed my undergraduate degree twenty-five years after I had started it.

The "motivational damage" I am referring to was preceded by various forms of disengagement. My practice of fauxchievement throughout my schooling was a symptom of disengagement. According to Gallup Student Poll data,[5] the national rate of student disengagement in the USA is rising. Each year hundreds of thousands of students in 5th to 12th grades are asked about their engagement in school. The students use a five-point scale to rate their agreement with nine items such as: "At this school, I

---

[4] For non-Americans readers, K-12 stands for Kindergarten through 12th grade, a.k.a primary and secondary schools.

[5] Gallup, 2011, 2012, 2013, 2014, 2015, 2016, 2017a (See References for full citations.)

get to do what I do best every day." "My teachers make me feel my schoolwork is important." "I feel safe in this school."[6] The data show that the rate of student disengagement steadily rose from 40% to 53% between 2011 and 2017. And they are not just a little bit disengaged; 9 of the 13 percentage points of the change are to the category Gallup calls "actively disengaged." This means that "they may be undermining the teaching and learning process for others."[7] The Carnegie Foundation for the Advancement of Teaching, a major source of funding for educational research and reform in the USA, issued a report called *Motivation Matters* that points out the importance and feasibility of solving these problems: "...[S]urveys have consistently identified an 'engagement gap' ... a divide that [some researchers] call 'both more pernicious and potentially more addressable' [than the achievement gap between racial minority and majority students in the USA]."[8]

Gallup's data may understate the impact of disengagement on students. We can estimate the rate by starting with a population of 58 million students and then assuming that 1) 7.14% will drop out,[9] 2) 25% of the remainder will graduate below basic standards,[10] and 3) 50-80% of the remainder will have been disengaged at a crucial point as noted by

Visualizing the Rates of Disengagement

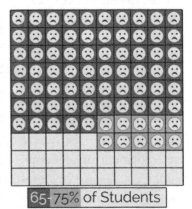

65-75% of Students

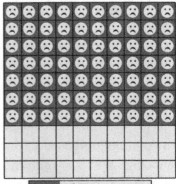

70% of Teachers

6 Gallup, 2018

7 Gallup, 2010

8 Headden & McKay, 2015

9 National Center for Education Statistics, 2016

10 Nord, Roey, Perkins, et al., 2011

DLAdvocates.org

Deeper Learning Advocates

Don Berg

Executive Director
Don.Berg@me.com
503-475-2158

If we can't reliably produce deeper learning in K-12 schools, then we are babysitting, not educating.

, 37.80 to 43.85 million students, a range of he total population, can be expected to be sengagement. Researchers at Gallup also say rted that they are disengaged.[12] This suggests nd teacher disengagement are roughly equal, h psychological research suggesting that d to engagement) is contagious.[13]

hat is confined to the schoolhouse. Gallup ally 85% of employees are disengaged and that ly $7 trillion in lost productivity.[14] Gallup also of disengaged teachers matches the rate of the rampant disengagement of the workforce everely underperforming if "career readiness" what we know about disengagement, we don't have a global productivity problem, we have a $7 trillion global learning problem.

My trajectory in K-12 enabled me to acquire and soon transcend the "Basics." "Back to Basics" is a school reform trope that is focused on delivering the 3R's of readin', 'ritin', and 'rithmetic; enforcement of "strict discipline;" and "no nonsense" in the classroom, as in no frivolous activities.[16] On the surface, it seems like a good idea, but problems arise from how we imagine it can be achieved. For some it conjures up a dream of getting children to attend something like a little schoolhouse on the prairie in a close-knit community that raised barns together before hiring a scholarly maiden school teacher to lovingly deliver those 3R's with a stick in hand. The romantic charm of this image is grounded in the reality that a quality education can be created only in a certain kind of place

11 Gardner, 2004 pp. 143-184

12 Hastings & Agrawal, 2015

13 Radel, Sarrazin, Legrain, & Wild, 2010

14 Harter, 2017

15 Hastings & Agrawal, 2015

16 Brodinsky, 1977; Weiss, 2016

where every child in the school has certain kinds of support. This is where the "system" becomes an important consideration.

The challenge we face is to figure out which kind(s) of support are necessary. Is it the focus on the 3R's, the feminine leadership, the threat of punishment, the accountability to the community, or something else altogether? If we pick out the wrong features to emphasize, then the truth is that even a little schoolhouse on the prairie can be a terrible place for learning. There are ways that even a small school in a close-knit community can undermine the kind of learning that is necessary in today's society. The idea of going "Back to Basics" has a certain appeal for addressing that wrongness I started sensing so long ago, but we must be careful about how we proceed or the wrongness will be perpetuated instead of eliminated when it is incorporated into "The System."

The System

Today the majority of children in the USA attend schools that are bureaucratic institutions embedded in urban communities populated with families who barely know their neighbors, quite the opposite of the romantic image of the little schoolhouse on the prairie. The based-on-a-true-story teacher movies *Stand and Deliver* (1988), *Dangerous Minds* (1995), *Music of the Heart* (1999), *The Ron Clark Story* (2006), *Freedom Writers* (2007), and *Beyond the Blackboard* (2011) portray multicultural cauldrons filled with masses of people barely putting up with, or even defying, their school bureaucracies. Documentaries celebrating great teachers in this vein include *Small Wonders* (1995), *OT- Our Town* (2002), *The Hobart Shakespeareans* (2004), *Touch of Greatness* (2004), *Mad Hot Ballroom* (2005), and *Class Act* (2005). Even rural schools today are coping with what were once thought of as "urban" problems. Ties to local, state, and federal governments may require rural schools to sacrifice some of the warmth and charm that might be imagined to occur in rural settings in the romanticized "back to basics" conception of schooling.

At the heart of every one of the movie stories are relationships among human beings who find ways to engage with each other and the reality of whatever they are learning. Within inner-city urban school bureaucracies there are ways to create opportunities for excellence, as

Movies Based on True Stories

attested to by the results that brought those real-life teachers to the attention of movie makers. The reason that those movies were made is that those teachers somehow tapped into the psychology of learning in spite of the pedagogical, curricular, disciplinary, and bureaucratic hurdles placed in their way. It is easy to miss what these very different stories all have in common. On the surface they are quite different. The kids are at elementary, middle, and high school levels. The range of subjects covers mathematics, English, music, drama, dancing, and more. The schools are all co-ed, but that's an irrelevant commonality. The secret to their success is engagement, for both teachers and students. The root cause of the failures that we care the most about is the opposite: *dis*engagement.

In each of the fictionalized movies, there are scenes and montages of short sequences that establish the climate of the school and/or class in which the main character is to perform their apparent miracle. Those establishing scenes put evidence of disengagement on obvious display. The students are variously bored, angry, defiant, and disruptively boisterous. They have no expectation that the teacher is capable of teaching them or that they are even capable of learning the subjects taught. They actively discourage the teacher and fellow students from being engaged with normal classroom processes. There are persistent threats of violence, in one form or another, even if only from the world outside the classroom.

The truth is that the central problem in our schools has little to do with academics and more to do with the psychology of learning. We will find the leverage we need to make a huge positive difference if we can focus on the psychological conditions for learning in schools by temporarily shifting our attention away from the pedagogical, curricular, disciplinary, and institutional details of schooling. There is actually something that inner-city schools *can* learn from the imaginary little schoolhouse on the prairie. But learning that lesson requires stripping away the surface features of the image to get at the psychological reality that is shared by all schools regardless of their context. The psychological reality that transcends all school contexts is the essential humanity of the students and teachers. (In my previous books I have presented behavioral and management strategies based on this reality.)[17]

The Missing Gauge

In the late 1990's a journalist asked me, "Why are you so angry?"

It was the first question in my first-ever one-on-one interview. I was surprised because I did not realize that what I had written about K-12 at the time came across that way. My goal since then has been to use that energy, but not the tone, to address the underlying systemic issues of schooling. If I am succeeding then the tone of my writing is no longer angry, but the intensity of my passion remains.

My struggle all these years has been to understand the *system* of education, not just the surface features of classroom-based schooling that usually dominate the discussion in popular media and the field itself.

---

[17] Berg & Allen, 2015; Berg, 2017

I have never been convinced that classroom instruction, per se, was a problem. What you are now reading is the result of my decades long intuition-inspired journey to understand education and its causes. If K-12 were a car, then the problem is that we measure land speed and engine speed (in the forms of grades and test scores, for instance) but don't have a gas gauge. School people do not seem to realize that the fuel for learning (motivation & engagement) is now measureable. The problems that arise from this lack of insight were not the result of conspiracy nor nefarious designs, they were caused by a combination of historical accidents, the unintended consequences of well-intentioned policies, and a fundamental misunderstanding of how education happens. The misunderstanding, embedded in policy, is that merely delivering knowledge, skills, and information can produce an education. This idea persists even though teachers know better; they were taught the truth in teacher school. As a result, too many teachers and students waste time and energy on policy-mandated unproductive activities only to run out of gas long before their journey is complete. Too many fall short of being properly educated.

Disengagement is a psychological challenge. It is *not* about the curriculum, the pedagogy, the disciplinary procedures, the institutional hurdles, or anything else that is usually blamed for the problems in the school system. As a student I did enough to get what I wanted out of the system, but not with enough engagement to actually master what I was taught.

From psychological research, we know how to produce engagement: support primary human needs. When students and teachers are put into situations in which their primary needs are met, then they willingly and joyfully engage with the activities available to them. After we get the psychological conditions right, then we will be far more effective at addressing the other issues. However, most people do not realize that primary human needs extend beyond air, water, food, shelter, and sleep to three additional psychological needs which I will discuss in more detail later.

The major challenge we face is how to flip the statistic from roughly 70% of students and teachers disengaged to engaging 70% or more. That can happen when school policies reflect the inherent constraints of the psychology of human engagement. Just as we already operate within many other inherent and imposed constraints that we don't think about, such as gravity, daylight, seasons, laws, budgets, schedules, calendars, etc., the same is true of school policies that can make teachers and students feel like pawns in other people's political games.

So, how do we get from here to there?

In literal car racing some very un-sexy things need to happen before the cars are ready for an exciting finish. We turn unsexy supply-chain processes (like extracting oil, refining it into fuel, and then delivering it to a raceway) into an awesome moment at the finish line by *managing* the car. The movement of the vehicle over land in miles per hour (mph) and the rotation of the engine in revolutions per minute (rpm) are apparently the *most* important information while driving. Displays of mph and rpm are two or three times larger than the gas gauge, which indicates a fuel level and/or the miles per gallon (mpg).[18] However, no fuel, no race. Fuel

18 Using the examples of a 2009 Honda Fit and a 1989 Chevy Corvette as representative examples shown above.

is crucial, despite the diminutive display. Imagine if cars did *not* have fuel gauges. Not impossible to manage, of course, but much more difficult and lots more people would make mistakes and run out of gas at inconvenient times and in potentially dangerous places.

Most schools understandably hope that test scores and grades will tell everyone everything they need to know about how well Johnny is learning and Jane is teaching. But there is nothing to indicate their fuel levels as they make that learning journey. In our race to educate citizens we naturally use test scores and grades to manage the system, but the fuel gauge is missing! The current system creates so much academic data that it can sometimes mask the human conditions that are actually shaping whether students and their teachers are successful.

Clearly we need to minimize shallow and fake learning and continue to reduce school-related violence (bullying, shootings, suicides, etc.). Howard Gardner noted in his book *The Unschooled Mind* that 50-80% of advanced degree holders are unable to answer the most basic questions in their field of specialty when asked in ways that are different from typical tests.[19] This indicates that while getting those advanced degrees their learning was shallow and the degrees reflect a significant degree of fauxchievement, not across-the-board mastery.

The National Center for Education Statistics reported in 2018 that, while overall rates of crime and violence are on the decline in K-12 schools, the mere presence of violence can "disrupt the educational process."[20] Test scores and grades do not provide the *right kind* of information to manage this complex *human* system. But, they *might* give us valuable insights into learning, **if** the un-sexy basics of being human are supported first.

In order to gauge the fuel for learning and teaching we need to know the psychological conditions of school environments, in particular the patterns of motivation and engagement there. Test scores and grades might still figure *most* prominently, like speedometers (mph) and

---

[19] Gardner, 2004 pp. 143-184

[20] Musu-Gillette, 2018

tachometers (rpm), but it is a particularly bad idea to continue turning a blind eye to the fuel for deeper learning.

Motivation and engagement are indirect indications that the primary human needs of the students and teachers are being met. You get good patterns of motivation and engagement only when primary human needs are adequately satisfied. The motivational damage I sustained in my K-12 schooling was because of the neglect of my psychological needs. The words "motivation" and "engagement" are just technical terms for the components that make up the *joy* in the title of this book: *More Joy More Genius*. My schooling robbed me of my joy. It is my fervent quest to prevent that from happening to any more children.

Spreading Psychological Innovations

There are schools leading the way, but some of the most promising models are not being given the right kinds of support to spread their psychologically relevant innovations. That's why I am writing this book. There is good stuff being done in the names of "the mentoring movement, a focus on the whole child, social emotional learning, character education, service learning, deeper learning, and national service"[21] but some schools implementing those models may still value academics at the expense of primary psychological needs. We won't know whether they are or not until data on the patterns of motivation and engagement in those schools are collected and published. Jal Mehta and Sarah Fine, in their book *In Search of Deeper Learning*, found that even

---

[21] AINCSEAD, 2018

in schools devoted to deeper learning there are some classroom teachers who fall back into ineffective teaching habits. They also found that in schools that have nothing to do with deeper learning there are usually at least a few teachers creating opportunities for excellence. The most consistent places where they found the kinds of pedagogical practice they were looking for were in extracurricular activities and elective classes. This incoherent pattern of practice is exactly why we need to find a way to gather appropriate data and manage accordingly.

There is a different set of schools that appear to make psychological need support more important than academics by making academic coursework optional; many of them call themselves "democratic" schools. Democratic schools are few and far between and only a vanishingly small proportion of them are publicly funded. If we can focus school reform efforts on the psychological principles that underlie learning, then more positive and lasting effects will result from promoting the school models that have already shown the way and transforming existing schools by implementing psychological innovations.

Mainstream schools do need to get back to basics. That is, back to being human in school, not *just* being academic. Academic tools like reading, writing, and arithmetic can express the goodness of our humanity. But academic tools can also become instruments of educational malpractice when primary human needs are thwarted instead of supported. The more we can help children and their teachers express joy in school, the more we will get to see their God-given genius there, too.

This book is organized into seven chapters, summarized below.

Chapter 1: Back to Basics, Version 2.0

Most K-12 schools inadvertently neglect psychological factors that significantly affect deeper learning. This is a problem because the increasing complexity and globalization of society necessitates deeper learning for good citizenship. School is the central institution for childhood education, but improving school systems requires setting up systematic feedback about the psychological conditions in schools, specifically how well primary human needs are supported. Support for primary human needs is a major determinant of the motivation and engagement of both students and teachers.

Chapter 2: Honoring the State's Interest in Learning

There are common sense, but questionable, assumptions behind the ways that some governments have used their coercive power to enforce school attendance. By taking a closer look at the assumptions that make those enforcement actions *seem* appropriate, we can acknowledge the State's interest in learning and reconsider how to honor the balance between the interests of States and parents.

Chapter 3: Iterating Toward Systematic Equity in Schools

When opportunities for strategic action arise, it is crucial that the changes being made are well designed from a human-centered perspective and that the design will be iterated over time to ensure that the experiences of the humans subjected to them are adequately taken into account. A set of design criteria modeled after another large-scale system is presented in order to encourage an appropriate design that promotes equity. Our transportation system has a more well-established track record for equitably meeting the needs of almost all of the people in our society and so serves as inspiration for the redesign of the education system.

Chapter 4: A Psychological Perspective on Human Nature

Developments in psychology have resulted in a fundamentally different notion of what a person is. The commonsense notion that we each have an atomistic individual mind with consistent specific character traits has not been helpful for creating robust and scientifically valid predictions of human behavior. The emerging view is that humans are embedded in and embodied by complex adaptive systems which make us relational beings with surprisingly flexible characteristics. This new view is changing how we understand the "self" and how it can inform our view of learning and education. This emerging view of human nature is crucial to understanding how the "hidden curriculum" of schools works and how we can mitigate the systemic detriments that it causes.

Chapter 5: The Psychological Foundations of Deeper Learning

The "Basic Psychological Needs" sub-theory of Self-Determination Theory suggests a theory of deeper learning. This proposed theory implies that systemic feedback about the psychological conditions in K-12 schools is lacking and needs to be established. A few tools are in use but more are needed. Existing assessments, which were developed for pure research, will need to be adapted and supported. If K-12 educators are to properly fulfill their duties to our children and to our society, they will need to use that feedback to understand that human existence and education are relational; education is not merely a series of discrete transactions (as in what Paulo Friere famously called "the banking model").

Chapter 6: E Pluribus Unum

The divisiveness of society presents a challenge to accomplishing substantial changes in the institutions that make it up. By drawing parallels with other field of human endeavor, we can start to see a way forward.

Chapter 7: A Policy Framework For Human Systems of Education

Practical change at the level of the large-scale system requires sustained attunement to opportunities at both the levels of organizations and society and strategic action in response. A policy resolution is proposed to orient activists to the central issues of deeper learning. Resolutions authorize stakeholders of all kinds to persistently bring up relevant issues over the long term. As warranted by the opportunities that arise, the stakeholders will be able to achieve either incremental adjustments or revolutionary shifts in laws, policies, and organizational habits.

I have been focused on the issue of improving K-12 education for decades. I have had an intuitive sense that something was fundamentally wrong in public schools ever since I was a student there. While working with private school children in the 1990's, I realized that the problem was pervasive in K-12 regardless of funding sources and management models. I have discovered that even the most promising of the currently available models of schooling do not fully address the fundamental psychological issue. It was only after getting my degree in psychology that I was able to really articulate what the fundamental issue is and how it provides a necessary critique for all forms of schooling in existence today. This book is the first time that my intuition about that wrongness has been properly articulated. Finally articulating it in a satisfying way also provided me with the inspiration to point you in the necessary direction to achieve the task of transforming the entire system.

Achieving The Impossible

To be clear, the task of total system transformation *is impossible* from your current vantage point. If I accomplish the core writer's task of communicating my point of view, then by the end of this book you will see that the impossibility is merely how it appears. You will see that while I provide neither a silver bullet nor a simple answer to a complex question, I am providing and pointing to navigational aids that can ensure that the direction we go is the *right* direction. The plan is to ensure that the changes we make are going to take advantage of a whole series of adjacent possibles that will eventually add up to accomplishing what currently *seems* impossible.

Everything that we have today that seemed impossible to someone in the past (space travel, cell phones, the eradication of smallpox, nuclear power, etc.) was arrived at through a series of adjacent possibles leading to the achievement of that seemingly impossible state of affairs. I first heard Stuart Kauffman's phrase "adjacent possible" in Steven Johnson's book *Where Good Ideas Come From.*[22] In the table above I present a set of

---

[22] Johnson, 2011

From The Actual To The Impossible	Actual "Now"	Adjacent Possible "Next"	Improbable "Later Maybe"	Impossible "Never"
Computing	1641 Computing By Hand	1642 Adding Machine	1940's Electronic Calculator	2007 iPhone
Transportation	1813 Horses	1814 Steam Trains	1885 Automobiles	1903 & 1961 Airplanes & Spacecraft
Communication	1829 Hand Delivery of Messages	1830's Telegraph	1876 Telephone	1895 & 1983 Radio & Internet
Medicine	1845 Miasma Theory of Disease	1846 Chlorinated Lime Hand Washing	1867 Antiseptic Surgery	1954 Organ Transplants

four examples of how our society has previously gone from a certain point in the past to arrive at some situation that was impossible at that prior moment. Each invention altered the probabilities and possibilities that were available in each of those arenas of human endeavor. Notice that the column labeled Actual "Now" contains dates that are the year prior to the column labeled Adjacent Possible "Next." The table is conveying the perspective from that "Now" on the later inventions that occurred. Once the invention occurs in the "Next" column then the possibilities and probabilities change. Johnson explained that innovation, whether it is biological or technological, necessarily proceeds from the now moment, which is completely constrained, into one of a large and also necessarily constrained (but not *as* constrained) number of next possible moments. That is how the previously impossible became possible, then probable, and finally actual.

My confidence that I am pointing you in the *right* direction comes from how I understand learning and more specifically how the science of psychology is articulating the foundations of it (even though psychologists do not label them as such). It turns out that recognizing the particular kind of human needs we have can provide us with exactly the guidance necessary to proceed as learners and teachers. If we can attune the system to what being human truly entails, then we will choose adjacent possibles that get us ever closer to the kind of education system that is today only an impossible pie-in-the-sky vision.

I used to be angry that I had my joy stolen. Later I was angry because I could see that incredible models and innovative practices were available yet nothing had really changed in schools-as-a-whole. This meant that the children I cared for were most likely to have their joy stolen, too. When I turned my attention to addressing the issues in K-12, I thought I should find someone to blame, someone who deserved to receive the brunt of my anger. As I continued to look closer and appreciate the complexity involved I found that everywhere I looked the people were doing their best with what they had. The truth is that I was wrong to look for someone to blame. The disengagement problem is real and immense, but no one created it on purpose. It is simply an unintended consequence of how the complex system we inherited is currently working.

The challenge is to join forces with those who are doing their best to care for students and teachers and empower them to express that caring more systematically. I trust that you are one of the caring people who just needs a little nudge in the right direction, in the direction of humanizing schools so that the joy expressed in kindergarten and first grade remains just as real and intense through eleventh and twelfth grades. Since motivation and engagement are contagious, achieving that outcome will require teachers to be passionate leaders and enthusiastic learners, too. The pie-in-*my*-sky right now is an entire system of enthusiastic students taught by passionate teachers in joyful K-12 schools. Since it is literally impossible for me to make that happen as an outsider to almost all schools, my aspiration is to be a catalyst that enables an educational leader like you to choose the adjacent possibles in your school or district that will bridge the gap between what is and what should be.

1 BACK TO BASICS, VERSION 2.0

While American schools are playing out a public policy obsession with content standards and testing, engagement is deteriorating.[23] Obviously, complete disengagement from learning (students dropping out and teacher turn-over) is bad, but less than complete disengagement is arguably a more significant problem. Teachers working in conditions that produce toxic stress and burn-out are disengaged. Children who are so unmotivated that they begin to disengage are not really learning the subjects they are being taught. They may get enough shallow knowledge to pass a test and/or get a passing grade, but they are still effectively ignorant.

For example, during my junior year (11th grade) in high school I had both semesters of math with Mr. Schuster and, based on my grades, did reasonably well. In June of that year I took the Scholastic Aptitude Test (SAT) for the first time. My best friend was one of several of my classmates in that college preparatory magnet program to get a perfect aggregate score of 1600. From within that comparison group my score of 1060 was not satisfactory, so I resolved to retake the test in December of my senior year (12th grade).

---

[23] Gallup, 2011, 2012, 2013, 2014, 2015, 2016, 2017a (See References for full citations.)

At the beginning of my senior year my new math teacher gave an assessment test. I failed it so completely that it was as if I had not taken Mr. Schuster's math classes. My teacher could not teach me two years at once nor could she transfer me out, so instead she assigned me to self-directed study of SAT preparation manuals. Test preparation manuals are *not* about the subject being tested, they are about the norms and conventions of testing.[24]

Since I was still being instructed in that subject, my English score should have improved much more than my math score. Instead, my English score only went from 560 to 610 while my math score went from 500 to 620, more than twice as much improvement without instruction. (The report from the College Board is shown below. The SAT scores are reported near the bottom left.) Plus, I got a passing grade for that junior year math class that I did not really take. Learning to master the norms and conventions of the testing process and passing classes without learning what was taught are forms of *fauxchievement*, that is, going through the motions without mastering the material. My learning may

---

ADMISSIONS TESTING PROGRAM
The College Board

COLLEGE PLANNING REPORT

SCORE REPORT FOR **DONALD   A BERG**   90713

Sex	Birth Date	Social Security No.	Telephone No.	Registration No.	Ethnic Group	U.S. Citizen	Report Date
M	1/21/68	– –	213-866-3122	7125119	White	Yes	2/08/86

High School Name and Code	First Language	Religion
LONG BEACH POLYTECHNIC HIGH SC 051480	English only	

JANUARY 1986 ACHIEVEMENT TESTS   Percentiles

Test	Score	Score Range 200 300 400 500 600 700 800	College-bound Seniors National State	National HS Sample
ENG COMP	570	<<<>>>	87	
MATH I	550	<<<>>>	51	

See the reverse side of this report for more information about these scores

SUMMARY OF TEST SCORES   Achievement Tests

Test Date	Grade Level	SAT Verbal	SAT Verbal Subscores Reading	Vocabulary	SAT Math	TSWE	Test Date	Grade Level	1	2	3
Dec 85 Jun 85	12th 11th	610 560	61 51	61 61	620 500	56 53	Jan 86	12th	EN 570	MI 550	

| | | | Average of All Reported Achievement Tests | 560 |

---

[24] *The Test and the Art of Thinking* is a feature length documentary that reveals the inner workings of test preparation professionals who freely admit that they are focused on norms and conventions of the tests, not the content. URL: http://TheTestDoc.org

have been deep with regard to the norms and conventions of the instructional situations and/or the testing regime, but it was shallow with regard to the realities of math; thus the ultimate educative purposes were defeated.

"Fauxcheivement" is a recently coined word in English, but the Chinese have had a term for the phenomenon for much longer. According to Yong Zhao[25] their term is:

> *Gaoten dineng*, which literally means high scores, but low ability. It is used to refer to students who score well on tests but have few skills that are usable in society. There are so many cases of "high scores, but low ability" that the term has been widely accepted as shorthand to describe education in China.

The problem of fauxchievement in science and math was taken up by a consortium made up of Harvard University, the Smithsonian Institution, Annenberg Media, and the National Science Foundation. They created two impressive suites of resources for the professional development of science teachers called *A Private Universe* in 1987 and *Minds of Our Own* in 1997. To illustrate their concern, they used the same demonstration for the opening sequences of the two video series they filmed. At the commencement ceremonies of MIT and Harvard they interviewed faculty and newly minted graduates. The interviewers asked them simple science and engineering questions about concepts that were covered in primary school. One question was, "Why are there seasons?" One challenge was having them light a small bulb using only a 9-volt battery and a single wire. The majority of the participants, regardless of their majors, were unable to answer the questions correctly or complete the tasks. Fauxchievement is a mild form of disengagement that is difficult to discern when the systems of grading and bureaucratic criteria for advancement allow students to use shallow subject knowledge to "pass" tests and "achieve" the benefits and rewards that should be reserved for those who have actually mastered the subject being taught.

---

[25] Zhao, 2009 p. 81

In his book *The Unschooled Mind*, Howard Gardner noted numerous studies showing that 50-80% of advanced degree holders (Bachelors to Doctorate) are unable to answer basic questions in their field of specialty when those questions were asked in a manner that is different from typical tests.[26] This fact implies that most advanced degree holders got their diplomas by practicing some level of fauxcheivement.

Heart of the Matter

Here's the simple but crucial question at the heart of the matter: What are the inputs that will produce the desired outcomes in education? Educational progressives talk about growth and use organic metaphors to suggest that learning must be cultivated like a garden. Educational traditionalists talk about delivering content and use mechanistic metaphors to suggest that learning can be managed with precision like a factory producing a car. It does not matter whether you favor organic or mechanistic metaphors to think about our systems for helping children learn; they will fall short if you don't know what outcomes are desirable and if you cannot identify the feedback you need to steer the system towards more reliably producing those outcomes. If the school system creates absurd situations for learning, like the ones in the scenarios presented later in this chapter, then there is a fundamental problem that goes beyond metaphors—a problem of educational malpractice.

The ever increasing complexity of our society has created ever more need for educated people. But, the process of learning that is at the heart of producing that result is stymied by a fundamental misunderstanding. If education policy-makers implicitly assume that teaching is as simple as delivering a package of content, they are inadvertently making a harmful error that confounds deeper learning.

The 2010 movie *Waiting for Superman* presented an animation with narration that made it clear that the filmmakers sincerely held this view. Two frames and the narration that went with that sequence are presented

---

[26] Gardner, 2004 pp. 143-184

Waiting for Superman on Teaching

Narrator: It should be simple. A
teacher in a schoolhouse filling
her students with knowledge
and sending them on their way.
But, we've made it complicated.

above. The idea continues to persist despite generations of notable educators criticizing the idea, such as Paulo Friere who derisively referred to it as the "banking model."

Most of the learning that made us successful over the last few thousand years did not require as much deep learning as today. Before the massive urbanization and industrialization of the last few hundred years, the majority of people were living in situations in which their intuitive default understandings were usually good enough to get by.

Most folks didn't need to have sophisticated understandings beyond what they could produce for themselves through direct contact with their trade and the community in which they lived. Industrial urban society in the past could afford to have an education system that was not very effective at facilitating deeper learning. As a system, it only had to ensure that a small proportion of the population would become people who could innovate; it did not need to be particularly good at it. However, it is now time to get straight about learning, adjust the feedback that guides the system, and become systematically more effective at getting all children to learn more deeply.

Imagine you are the ultimate master teacher with a perfectly planned math lesson. What do you think about these five learning scenarios?

- Ravish is a shy seventeen-year-old from an extremely wealthy family. On a family trip to the International Space Station he is taking his lesson outside without a spacesuit or breathing equipment. Will the lack of atmosphere influence his learning?

- Heath is an outgoing thirteen-year-old from a middle class family. He is a wrestler who has been dehydrating himself for several days in order to make a lower weight class for a match. Is he ready to learn deeply?

- Wing is a homeless ten-year-old. Her last "meal" was a bag of potato chips a few days ago. What are the odds she'll master the lesson?

- What if a new policy dictated teaching students in a local wilderness area while everyone is naked in a blizzard?

- The budget has been cut; how about a 45-day school year where you teach an entire year's worth of content non-stop for 1,080 hours (180-day school year x 6 hours per day)?

No matter how perfect the lessons and/or the teacher, there are things on the human side of the schooling equation that can negate everything on the academic side. I assume that you recognize suffocation, dehydration, starvation, exposure, and lack of sleep as fundamental barriers to learning. Further I assume that you share my moral sense that they would be intolerable expedients in the event someone were to propose the idea of using them as means to some noble goal involving children. Three more scenarios presented later in this chapter are similarly constructed, but seem to be generally accepted as normal in K-12. That acceptance is a significant problem since it is likely responsible for the pervasive pattern of disengagement I mentioned in the introduction. I assume that no one in their right mind would advocate for a school system that does harm to some children and teachers *by design*. Therefore, while it is possible that some degree of *inadvertent* harm may be inevitable in such a large-scale system, I am not interested in positing some amount of harm that might be *necessary* to achieve a greater good. All eight scenarios (five above, three to come) illustrate the thwarting of primary human needs and by definition they represent situations that are harmful to learning, and therefore, even if they were an expedient means to some end, they would be morally outrageous, and must be prevented.

The first four scenarios above depict *physiological* needs; if you are deprived of them for long enough, you die. The fifth one above and the three presented later depict *psychological* needs. An unfortunate natural experiment in the 1940's involving the institutionalization of infants can help us understand the importance of fulfilling psychological needs.[27] The researchers observed 91 infants abandoned at a foundling home and 220 infants at a prison nursery, separated from their mothers. In the foundling home each nurse had to manage 8 to 12 infants, allowing only the absolute minimum of care. The observers noted that the children in the foundling home "got about one-tenth of the normal affective supplies provided in the usual mother-child relationship." I interpret that observation to indicate a generalized neglect of their primary psychological needs, an idea that had not yet been articulated. They also noted that the *physical* conditions of the foundling home were *superior* to that of the prison nursery. In the prison nursery the infants were living in similarly institutional conditions except for the addition of "mothering" by someone other than their biological mother. In the

---

[27] Spitz, 1965

prison nursery during the first two years less than 1% of the children (2 out of 220) died, while in the physically superior facility the foundling death rate was 37.3% (34 out of 91). The children who survived the foundling home were also severely diminished in *all* their capabilities.

This discrepancy in outcomes resulted from the behavioral guidance provided by the interaction between the institutional policies and the human brains in those situations. The responsible policy-makers assumed that the foundlings could be managed like a bunch of mechanical robots on maintenance schedules. Given the system created by the policies, the nurses could attend only to the most minimal physiological needs of the infants and not to their psychological needs. In this case, the policies regarding the foundlings were pervasively harmful; many died and the survivors were left with lifelong learning difficulties. The regulations that now apply to institutionalized children recognize that insufficient support for psychological needs is intolerable as a means to management expedience because the well-being of both the children and the adults caring for them are at stake.

The learning scenarios I'm presenting in this chapter reflect this potential for harm. When setting the scenes above, some details were thrown in just to evoke irrelevant ideation. The only fact that matters is the humanity of the people involved. The humanity of learners and teachers is also the only relevant fact we need in order to conclude that learning will be diminished, perhaps severely, when psychological needs are thwarted. Thwarting of psychological needs usually won't kill teachers nor school-age children, but it will diminish their engagement.

Thwarting Psychological Needs

The reason that it is utterly foolish to even suggest that we could pack a whole year of learning into an instructional marathon of about a thousand consecutive hours is that we need to sleep. Sleep is the most obvious psychological need we have. Sleep deprivation is hazardous to both physical and mental health and the results can be severely harmful, though there is no credible evidence for the possibility of dying from it. Sleep deprivation can be a significant contributing factor to any number of accidents or dysfunctions that may cause death, but it is not the sleep deprivation itself that will kill you. The symptoms of sleep deprivation include various forms of psychological distress, such as anxiety and depression. The three scenarios presented later are based on three other psychological needs that also produce those kinds of symptoms; thwarting them should be considered equally absurd in terms of their impact on the learning process.

In Self-Determination Theory, the leading theory of human motivation in psychology, there were initially three criteria for classifying a need as primary (more have been developed). The key initial criteria were 1) the effects of a need cannot be neutral with regard to well-being, 2) it had to apply cross-culturally, and 3) the need cannot be derived from other needs.[28] Non-neutrality means that meeting a need has to have a positive effect on well-being while thwarting it has a negative effect. The cross-cultural requirement means that there cannot be any human beings who have well-being without it. Finally, needs that naturally follow from other needs are secondary or derivative, not primary. The primary needs presented here have robust scientific support according to these criteria and that makes it clear why various "needs" proposed by others (e.g. Maslow's "Hierarchy") are not included—more on that later.

To better understand the relationship between primary and other kinds of needs and how they work together to generate our experiences of the world, consider the relationship between letters of the alphabet and how they work together to generate the literature we enjoy. There are two basic categories of the letters I know how to use: vowels and consonants. A vowel is required to form almost all words[29] and all the different letters appear with different frequencies in various words and those words also vary in frequency of use. Another important fact about this alphabet is that there are distinct cultural differences in how it is used in the different Western European languages that share it. The key point of this analogy is that the needs are a generative structure that combine to make up larger structures that inform how we experience the world. It would not make any sense to make the claim that there is a hierarchy

---

[28] Baard, Deci, & Ryan 2004; Deci & Ryan 2000; Ryan & Deci 2000a; Ryan & Deci 2006

[29] Except for a variety of interjections (hm, psst, shh, etc.), the words tsktsk and nth (as in "to the nth degree") are the most commonly used vowelless words in contemporary English.

of letters or words and that the use of some depends on the use of others. Just because there happen to be vowels in nearly every word does not mean that there is a hierarchical relationship between vowels and consonants. There is a higher frequency of some letters but that does not create a dependency relationship between them.

Primary human needs are similarly generative structural elements. Primary needs are the components (memetic letters) that make up the literature of all human experiences. The physiological needs are like vowels while the psychological needs are like consonants. While it is true that the primary physiological needs are necessarily addressed more frequently, that fact does not create a dependency relation among the needs themselves.

Despite having created a truly compelling image that will likely go on misleading people for many more years to come, this is where Maslow got it wrong. The research into primary psychological needs has shown that they are interrelated, but not hierarchical.[30] For instance, let's consider the student in the scenario presented above about the need for water. We can reasonably expect that the dehydrating wrestler would be able to function for some time as a human being even if his functioning as a student would deteriorate. His learning would get shallower, but his dehydration was accomplishing a purpose that he valued. If Maslow was right, then we should be expecting him to have ceased to be a functional human being before he could accomplish his purpose. If a hierarchical relation existed, his dehydration, the thwarting of a "lower" need, should have precluded his desire to achieve the "higher" need.

The truth is that we have a memetic alphabet of primary needs that get mixed and matched in distinct personal and cultural patterns that generate human experiences. Some of the needs Maslow hypothesized, like self-actualization and esteem, are better thought of as words or paragraphs that are culturally shaped derivatives of the primary needs. It will not do any harm to pursue derivative needs, but it would be a mistake to use Maslow's notion of hierarchical relations among the needs.

---

[30] Ryan & Deci, 2000a

In schooling, the lack of hierarchical relations is particularly important to understand due to the ways that the traditional notion of "back to basics" tends to be implemented. The basics are typically delivered by simplistic rote learning processes in which students and teachers find little to no meaning. The typical characterization of it as "drill and kill" is telling. Drills are fine, except when they involve the "kill" bit. Meaningfulness happens to be a derivative need.[31] Those curricular and pedagogical choices made under the spell of a "back to basics" mantra will tend to preclude enabling children to do activities they personally find meaningful until *after* they have acquired the "basics."[32] The meaninglessness of those activities will cause their learning to be shallower than it otherwise could have been and, because of negative associations arising from being coerced into doing them, could delay their acquisition of those skills. The meaninglessness is derived from the neglect or thwarting of the teachers' and children's primary psychological needs, described below. Meaninglessness does educational harm, even in the absence of any other observable sources of physical or emotional harm. Striking the right balance between the student's relationship to the subject and their competence in it is crucial to deeper learning.

The Combinatorial Systems Table on the next page extends the idea of the alphabet of needs in order to compare it with both the prototype of the alphabet but also with an already well established scientific analogy; the biological system of genetics. With that said, let's complete the list of primary needs.

The three additional primary human needs that most people are unfamiliar with are autonomy, relatedness, and competence. Having those three psychological needs satisfied (along with the other five needs) puts a learner in the right state of mind to learn deeply. In order for us to be on track towards systematically facilitating deeper learning, the following three scenarios need to be automatically understood as antithetical to it:

---

[31] Martela, Ryan & Steger, 2017

[32] Mehta, 2018

Combinatorial Systems

Prototype	Established Example	Proposed Example
Written Language	Central Dogma of Biology	Social/ Mind Sciences
Alphabet	Base Molecules	Primary Needs
Punctuation	Stop Codons	Secondary Needs
Words	Genes	Behaviors, Derivative Needs
Sentences	Chromosomes	Activities
Paragraphs	Genomes	Roles
Chapters	Organs	Norms/ Laws/ Policies
Books	Organisms	Groups/ Organizations/ Institutions
Libraries	Ecologies	Cultures/ Societies

Julz is not allowed to make meaningful choices about her own activities.

This scenario is about the primary need for *autonomy*. Psychologist Daniel Gilbert[33] reported on the importance of this need in elderly adults in reference to a study by Richard Schulz and Barbara Hanusa.[34]

> The fact is that human beings come into the world with a passion for control, they go out of the world

---

[33] Gilbert, 2006

[34] Schulz & Hanusa, 1978 pp. 22-23

the same way, and research suggests that if they lose their ability to control things at any point between their entrance and the exit, they become unhappy, helpless, hopeless, and depressed. And occasionally dead. … [T]he importance of perceived control for the welfare of nursing home residents [was studied] but had an unexpected and unfortunate end [because] a disproportionate number of residents who had been in the high-control group had died.

The "high-control group" were the ones who had their need for autonomy supported. After the study ended and that support was no longer available, they suffered and more of them died than in the comparison group.

Autonomy, for me as a member of an individualist culture, is largely conflated with making my own choices. However, research suggests it is more nuanced than merely choice making. What is most important is not the identity of the decision maker, but the relationship *to* the decision maker. A study of Chinese children showed that a particularly strong relationship, such as with the child's mother or teacher, can cause a child to feel that doing the activity chosen by that other person is almost as autonomous as one chosen directly by the child.[35] The need for autonomy can only be satisfied by people the child trusts and it just so happens that children trust themselves more than anybody else. And it may be that, unlike some of the Chinese children studied, American children are chronically distrustful of adults.

Miguel does not trust his teacher and/or his classmates.

If Miguel were in a school that accepted learning situations like the wilderness class in a blizzard, he would be quite right not to trust an adult who is willing to let him freeze. But, the issue is more complicated than that. The primary human need at stake here is *relatedness*. Relatedness means a combination of having a sense that you belong and that you are

---

[35] Bao & Lam, 2008

recognized by others for being yourself.[36] When that is the case then trust tends to follow. This is something that is likely to be realized differently based on the cultural context in which the child is situated. The University of Hong Kong's Xue-Hua Bao and Shui-Fong Lam studied how motivated school children were for activities that the experimenters told them were chosen for them by their peers, their teacher, or their mother. The children with especially strong relationships with their mother or teacher perceived the activity to be almost as autonomous as those who had made the choice themselves. The results suggest to me that collectivist cultures may provide more support for children to have positive relationships with authority (mother and teacher) than individualist cultures.

We humans always face the question of whether an authority is trustworthy or not. A culture can provide a default tendency one way or another but the individual must ultimately decide what behavior is appropriate. The relationships among students and teachers must involve some degree of trust or they will not be able to attain the openness required for deeper learning. But even if the student develops a trusting relationship with their teacher, the influence of untrustworthy peers can still destroy many opportunities for deeper learning. Trust (a derivative of relatedness) must be pervasive in the classroom in order to create a consistently productive deeper learning environment.

Donald is not getting informative feedback from the reality of the subject matter he is studying.

This scenario is about the primary need for *competence*. Donald needs information from the reality that underlies the subject being taught. Recall my math experiences in high school. Sustained and meaningful engagement with the mathematical world was absent; I was missing feedback about my ability to operate effectively within that world. It is not enough for a student to cleverly arrange words or other symbols that relate to the subject matter according to production rules in his/her head, like I did for Mr. Schuster. When I studied math again over 20 years later

---

36 Ryan & Deci, 2006

in the process of finishing my undergraduate degree I was better connected to the reality and more successful as a learner. The mere arrangement of symbols does not affect the mental mappings of the reality of a subject. Only active engagement with that reality and getting good feedback from it (or accurate simulations of it) will alter a student's mental map appropriately (more on this in Chapter 2).

To return to the example of "old school" back to basics version 1.0 reform, if a school policy ignores the importance of relevance, then children are unlikely to feel that their identity has been incorporated into the decision making process. Consequently, the children will feel that the activities they are made to do are not really helping them to achieve *their* goals and aspirations.

There is a common refrain that I have heard from adults who are skeptical of giving children too much say in what they will do at school. They will jump to the conclusion that I am using "psychological need support" as a code to advocate for all schools becoming laissez faire, free-for-all anarchies in which teachers are expected to pander to the whims of the children. They will note that I hold up some schools that call themselves "free schools" as exemplars even though the majority of similar schools that came into existence over the past hundred years have failed (i.e. ceased to exist). Their response will be along the lines of, "Children are too immature to understand what they will need to be successful in the future; they have to learn to do things that they don't want to do. Some things are just too important to leave to the whims of children." Or the more sophisticated might complain that, "Children need structure." In essence, if they are educational conservatives they might accuse me of putting the failed wolf of "progressive education" in a sheep's clothing of psychology.

Out of respect for their underlying concern, which is legitimate, I will just say that while I generally self-identify with and, personally, prefer the progressive side of the educational philosophy spectrum, I am more committed to the science-based position that primary psychological need support leads to better motivation and engagement, which in turn leads to the best possible educational outcomes. If the "traditional" pedagogical practices that educational conservatives prefer can be practiced in a manner that is consistent with primary human need support, then that's great. I'm all for it, even if I don't like it.

In fact, when I did my thesis research on patterns of motivation in two alternative private K-12 schools, I asked to interview teachers with experience in both traditional and alternative schooling. In the interviews I always asked them about the differences between those contexts. One teacher at the home school resource center, which operates like community college but for pre-kindergarten through twelfth grade, said that during her multi-decade career as a very traditional public school math teacher she had objected to home schooling. But, after retiring and being recruited to teach at the home school resource center she discovered the error of her ways. And more to my point, she said that everything she did in her classes was the same. She *taught* just as traditionally as she had before. The main differences were that she had a broader range of ages in classes, the kids had all chosen to be there, and that the school administration trusted her more as a professional. My research suggested that both the home school resource center and the democratic "free school" that I studied maintained the intrinsic motivation of their students. That result stands in stark contrast to over 30 years of data in which all the mainstream schools show declines in intrinsic motivation or engagement within and across years. Since motivation is a down-stream effect of primary need support, then those schools did a better job of providing need support than traditional schools.

Even though "over 30 years of data" sounds impressive, it represents merely dozens of studies that have all been conducted since the 1980's and 90's when relevant measures were being developed and scientifically validated. More importantly, it largely excludes schools that are devoted to deeper learning, democratic/free schools, home school resource centers, and other innovations that may hold the keys to providing better need support and sustainably engaging students. We just have not gotten enough scientifically valid feedback about the psychological conditions in schools to know for certain whether some pedagogies, curricula, institutional arrangements, disciplinary practices, etc. are better than others.

I respect the underlying concern that is expressed by educational conservativism. Conservatives are correct that chaos is not helpful and that children need structure. However, there are many different kinds of structure. If they insist that children need academic structure more than social structures, then we have a more fundamental disagreement. What the most "radical" schools that I have studied, and tend to personally favor, do is to provide clear and compelling social structures to the point of making academic structures available only as opt-in choices for children. In order to have a productive debate about the relative value of academic structures, the champions of educational conservativism need to be clear about what they are promoting as the social structure in which their favored academic structures are implemented. I am pointing out that psychological reality makes the social structure, as defined by how it supports, neglects, or thwarts primary human needs, far more educationally powerful than all academic structures. If we don't get the social structures aligned with the support of primary needs, our efforts will be generally ineffective no matter what academic structure is put in place.

To be clear about the relationship between different types of needs consider the diagram on page 38. The organizing principle of the diagram is that primary needs have non-neutral effects on well-being. When they are supported, as shown by the black arrows pointing down to the left side of the bottom bubble, there is an increase in well-being. Secondary needs are ones that make a unique contribution to well-being beyond what primary needs provide, but there is no decrease in well-being if secondary needs are thwarted. When primary need are thwarted there is a decrease in well-being, shown by the gray arrow pointing down to the right side of the bottom bubble. Derivative needs are those that make no unique contribution beyond what primary needs provide to well-being. The diagram indicate derivation by the bubble in the middle that intercepts both of the arrows from primary needs on their way to the well-being bubble. Urinating and defecating are crucial to well-being, but they are derivative from our needs for food and water. Recent research has suggested that beneficence is a secondary need[37] and that meaningfulness is a derivative need.[38]

Using the alphabet metaphor derivative needs are like words and secondary needs are punctuation. When you mix and match the letters in an orderly way you make words. When you add punctuation then there is more clarity about how to parse and process the words that are given. Punctuation uniquely adds to the reader's ability to understand how the author is using the alphabet to make words and sentences.

We cannot guide ourselves nor our systems properly if we are not attuned to the right feedback. Good feedback is an issue for our whole system, not just the individuals within it. A child needs feedback about how the subject they are studying relates to the reality that underlies that subject. A school organization needs feedback about how the educational services they provide relate to the reality of learning that underlies the student's experience of that school. The society needs feedback about how the student, the school, and the society align with each other on supporting or thwarting needs at each level. Schools that undermine the needs of children are warping the mental maps of citizenship that those children are developing. Those mental maps are going to be the basis for their later workplace and adult citizenship behavior. When the school distorts the child's perceptions in a way that results in shallow and fake learning then the child is necessarily out of touch with reality and is less likely to be successful in the long run. That mental mapping process necessarily starts in the family and then progresses (or regresses) in school.

Vulnerable populations can be significantly harmed by the neglect or denial of support for their psychological needs. It usually won't kill most schoolchildren or their teachers, but the potential for harm is real and has lasting effects. Deeper learning aside, the harm being inflicted on children is a grave outcome that no one ever wanted from our school system.

---

[37] Martela & Ryan, 2016. The cited paper does not present the evidence that downgraded beneficence, I heard the news when Richard Ryan announced it from the stage at the 6th International Self-Determination Theory Conference in 2019.

[38] Martela, Ryan & Steger, 2017

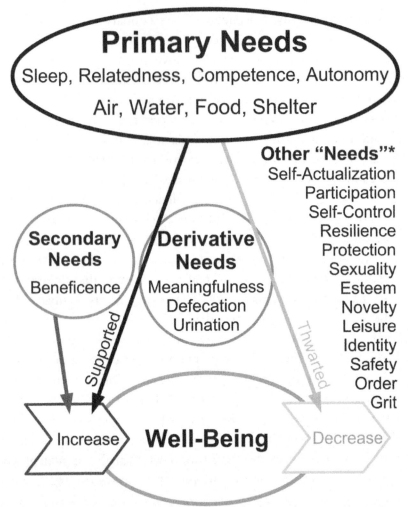

* This list includes needs proposed by Abraham Maslow, Manfred Max-Neef, the NVC community, and others. They are probably mostly derivative, but some may be secondary. Scientific research is needed for proper classification (which will include calling some too vague to be useful, e.g. self-actualization.)

It is time to get back to basics but we need a new version of what we count as "basic." It is time for Back to Basics version 2.0, where we get down to the basics of being human before tackling the basics of being academic. In the global society we have inherited from our ancestors, deeper learning is increasingly necessary for long-term success. In the following chapters it will become clear that Back to Basics v2.0 requires three things of school leaders:

1. Teach governance before academics.
2. Manage for engagement, not obedience.
3. When things get hard, provide more support, not less.

These are the strategies that I have come to believe will produce deeper learning more consistently.

Before you can reach the same conclusion I need to set more of the context in which I am thinking about these issues. In the next chapter I will call into question how we, as members of powerful States with significant interests in the education of children, think about collectively acting on those interests. What would it mean to align the more natural interests of parents and our society to achieve that same outcome. Let's explore how the State's interest in education interacts with parent's interests in their child's well-being.

2 HONORING THE STATE'S INTEREST IN LEARNING

If a parent chooses to take personal responsibility for their child's learning, in some parts of the world they could be at risk of criminal prosecution or of having their children kidnapped by the government. Here are some headlines that reflect this concern:

- 2019 USA: Mom Arrested and Booked for Homeschooling[39]
- 2018 Norway: Homeschooled Boy Tackled by Police[40]
- 2017 Cuba: Cuban Pastor Jailed for Homeschooling[41]
- 2017 USA: Was Buffalo Mom Jailed Over Homeschooling Decision?[42]
- 2017 Germany: German Parents Go To Court After Police Seize Kids Over Homeschooling[43]

---

[39] https://hslda.org/content/hs/state/ms/20190204-mom-arrested-and-booked-for-homeschooling.aspx

[40] https://hslda.org/content/hs/international/Norway/20180214-homeschooled-boy-tackled-by-police.aspx

[41] https://hslda.org/content/docs/media/2017/201704270.asp

[42] https://www.wkbw.com/news/was-buffalo-mom-jailed-over-homeschooling-decision

[43] https://www.thelocal.de/20170406/german-parents-go-to-eu-court-after-police-seized-kids-

- 2010 Brazil: Brazilian Couple Receive Criminal Conviction for Homeschooling[44]
- 2007 Germany: Homeschooler Flees State Custody[45]
- 2006 Australia: Government Interference: The Tale of [the Closure of] Booroobin Sudbury School in Queensland[46]

These are just the most extreme examples of how, just because parents act on the assumption that they have prior claim to educating their children, states can act very aggressively to protect their interests in children's education. What could possibly drive otherwise caring people in control of government laws and their enforcement to unleash their massive coercive power against innocent children and otherwise law-abiding and well-intentioned parents? I suspect it is their assumptions about learning and the state's interest in it.

Examining The State's Interest in Learning

The only sense I see behind compulsory school attendance laws and their enforcement is the following suite of four ideas:

1. certain kinds of experiences are better than others for immature people, specifically, children
2. the state has a substantial vested interest in the kinds of experiences that are made available to children as they are growing up
3. activities or materials that are labeled "educational" by authorized groups or individuals are the kinds of experiences that are better for children, and

---

in-homeschool-raid

[44] https://www.lifesitenews.com/news/brazilian-couple-receive-criminal-conviction-for-homeschooling

[45] https://www.wnd.com/2007/04/41250/

[46] https://www.libed.org.uk/index.php/reviews/178-articles/349-government-interference-the-tale-of-booroobin-sudbury-school-in-queensland

4. the full force of the government should be used to ensure that all children are made to do the activities that are officially labeled "educational"

    (Most countries have conceded that parents and non-governmental organizations are capable of providing "educational" activities, so they allow homeschooling and a variety of school organizations to exist as long as they do "educational" activities, with some glaring exceptions as the incidents above illustrate.)

I agree with, and do not question, the first and second assumptions. It is the third and fourth assumptions that are problematic in the face of what is known about learning.

Mainstream schools are conceived, organized, operated, evaluated and defended as necessary because (it is assumed) normal people, especially immature people like children, cannot, and/or will not, learn to be successful unless they are made to go to school. The majority of schools in the world today act as if learning is deliberate, effortful and avoidable.

What is now known is that exactly the opposite, however, is also true; learning is also automatic, unconscious and impossible to avoid. You are probably wondering how it can be both, so give me a chance to explain. Learning is, in fact, a property of all living things. To be alive implies it. The only time you stop it is when you sleep, get very ill, or die.

"But," a skeptic replies, "if that's true then how come some kids go through years of schooling without learning to read and write?" This retort is misleading despite the fact that the concern behind it is well founded. Let's consider "seeing" as a parallel to "learning." For example, how is it that some blind people automatically react to visual cues that they can't see?

Researchers have discovered that in certain kinds of blindness the subjects retain some automatic visual functions, despite their complete inability to "see" normally.[47] When an accident or disease damages certain parts of their brains these people cannot see in our normal sense of the

---

[47] See: https://www.scientificamerican.com/article/when-blindness-is-in-the-mind/

term, but their eyes and other parts of their visual systems still work. So, they can still react automatically and unconsciously to certain kinds of visual stimuli. It's a phenomena known as "blind-sight." Despite the fact that some aspects of their visual systems are working, these people do not have the ability to direct their attention to that information. Most of the components of their visual system are still operating, but the only operational functions are non-conscious and automatic.

Given these observations and their implications for what we know about "seeing," then consider the statement, "As long as your eyes are open then seeing is automatic, unconscious, and impossible to avoid, but seeing the letters in this sentence is deliberate, effortful, and avoidable." This statement is true but it applies two apparently contradictory descriptions to the phenomenon of sight. The crucial difference between the two descriptions of sight is the general verb "seeing" and the specific verb clause "seeing the letters in this sentence." The general verb is referring to the over-all process that occurs when visual information is available whereas the specific verb clause is referring to the necessity of directing attention in order for that automatic, unconscious, and unavoidable process to act upon specific visual information.

Daniel Kahneman's book *Thinking Fast & Slow* provides a good summary of the evidence for the nature of learning. Kahneman was one of the researchers who first uncovered how irrational people can be when they are presented choices in a manner that exploits certain features of how our minds work. The title of his book, *Thinking Fast & Slow*, refers to how the two aspects of our minds work in different ways. The "logical" part tends to be slow while the "emotional" part tends to be fast. It was previously assumed that we are mostly logical unless a situation became intensely emotional. But what he found out over the course of his long career is that we are mostly going to think fast and those fast decisions are only going to be as good as the training that shapes them. If the training is done in direct contact with reality and is shaped by slow processes of reflection on the feedback that is received from reality, then the decisions that result are more likely to be good. The truth is that all logical thought is informed by emotions, so pitting "logical" thought against "emotional" thought is a crock. The challenge is not to choose one over the other, the challenge is to know when and how to deploy your thinking tools appropriately. Learning is both fast (automatic, unconscious, and unavoidable) and slow (deliberate, effortful, and avoidable). It is the deployment of both fast and slow thinking that is going to be most valuable for effective learning.[48]

Now reconsider the skeptic's implicitly critical retort to my description of "learning" given that the statement I made is about the general verb and his retort is about specific learning tasks. This skeptic's concern is actually well founded, in so far as it is true that many children remain illiterate despite attending school. For example, in the book *Why cant U teach me 2 read?* Beth Fertig[49] wrote about a group of students in New York who sued the school system for failing to teach them to read. She points out in the book that these children were typical of many former students except for the fact that they sought a legal remedy.

Returning to the list at the beginning of this section, we have all accepted assumption number two that we, as components of the state, share in a vested interest in the successful education of those children. But the fact of illiteracy does not falsify the statement about learning being automatic; it is really a non-sequitor. In fact, learning to read and write are both deliberate, effortful and avoidable tasks, just like seeing the letters in this sentence. The problem is not the learning process, the problem is with the way children deliberate on, apply effort to, and avoid those specific activities.

I have, at this point, admitted that some children avoid those activities and appear to have justified the necessity of the fourth assumption (regarding enforced schooling for all). But, we have not yet addressed the third idea upon which the fourth is based, and to address the skeptic's concern properly, it is crucial to answer the following question first: If

---

[48] This is also the conclusion reached by Gary Klein (1999, 2011) who was at one time Kahneman's rival in the field of decision-making research. They ended up collaborating for many years and ultimately reconciled their apparent differences of opinion by realizing they were studying fundamentally different situations. Klein's initial view developed from the study of experts while Kahneman's came from studying novices. (See References for full citations.)

[49] Fertig, 2009

learning is automatic, unconscious, and impossible to avoid, then what were all those illiterate students learning while their teachers were trying unsuccessfully to teach them to read and write?

They were learning the same things that every single experience you have while you are alive teaches you:

1. how to manage your own and other people's behavior,
2. what you exchange with your environment, and how you exchange it, to meet your own and other people's needs, and
3. the patterns of consciousness that result from being embedded in those power structures for managing behavior and those exchange processes for meeting needs.

What those children learned was the "hidden curriculum." They learned that their opinions about what is worth paying attention to are not important. They learned that their obedience to authority is more important than meeting their fundamental needs. And a number of other lessons including those that late multiple award-winning teacher John Taylor Gatto talked about in his book *Dumbing Us Down*.

From this perspective, what counts as "educational" is not an objective feature of any particular set of materials or activities; it is a property that emerges out of the process of each student choosing a certain depth of connection to their own experiences.

Determining the "educational" value of something depends on what you mean by the term. Of course, "educational" activities are those that are supposed to produce an educated person. But for many people an "educated person" is simply someone who has successfully jumped through all the hoops that schools put in front of them.

Others take great pains to list out particular knowledge, skills and information that are typically possessed, or should be possessed, by an "educated person" (e.g. E.D. Hirsch, the education conservative who famously wrote a series of books that claims to spell out exactly what every American child "needs to know" at each grade level from preschool to sixth grade). Then they make great efforts to ensure that their list is officially authorized to become the set of hoops that schools put in front of children. I call this the education-as-symbol-manipulation position, and if you take it to be the whole extent of what counts as "educational" then you will probably take the third and fourth assumptions to be self-evident and beyond criticism. And you would be *logically* correct in taking that position, based on what you consider to be an "educated person." Let's consider the "educational" value of reading Shakespeare or Confucius, as examples. It would simply be a matter of determining if people who are already considered "educated" have read them, then getting the educational experts to agree that reading those works must have contributed to the production of their "education" (with appropriate analysis of how Shakespeare or Confucius must have stimulated certain skills and abilities and contributed to the knowledge they possess).

Finally, those experts would officially declare that reading the works of Shakespeare or Confucius is an objectively "educational" activity based on their rigorous studies. As a matter of fact, you will probably find reading Shakespeare on every English speaking education expert's list of "educational" activities, ditto for Chinese speaking experts and Confucius. And I suspect, though I have not looked into it, that every English or Chinese speaking government that has issued "education" standards includes reading them, too.

On the other hand, I assert that an "educated person" is better defined as someone who is able to perceive accurately, think clearly, act effectively on self-selected goals and aspirations, and engage in an on-going process of cognitive cartography in which they map out their experiences and their relationship to reality as they understand it. Taking this definition of education means that symbol manipulation is not the central defining feature of what it means to be educated. The central defining feature of being "educated" involves engagement with a learning process connected to your current life situation as defined by your own goals and aspirations, thus demoting symbol manipulation to the subservient position of one of many tools available for creating experiences and relating them to each other. This is what I call the education-as-attitude position.

Given the education-as-attitude position, then what is "educational" is dependent on each individual student's situation in time and space plus what his/her different choices in the past and future mean in relation to their current goals and aspirations. These are entirely unique to each individual and cannot be predicted or controlled by anyone else. What makes any experience "educational" is an emergent property of how the complex adaptive individual interacts with their complex adaptive environment.

For instance, the idea that reading Shakespeare or any other author is inherently "educational" is, from this perspective, absurd. It *could* be educational if, and only if, the learner actually chooses to put effort into associating other experiences in their life and current situation with the world that Shakespeare creates with words such that Shakespeare's perspective contributes to his/her cognitive maps of reality.

Consider the situation of making students in three different states of mind read Shakespeare. The first set are students who have experienced something bad; they're traumatized. The second set are students who have not been experiencing anything good nor particularly bad in their lives; they're bored. Finally, there are the students who are enthusiastic; it's all good to them. The simple point is that the traumatized and bored students cannot learn deeply, while the enthusiastic students can. The Causal Storylines for Education table on the next page shows the chains of events that are predicted by these two views of education.

Shakespeare's words have been powerful in helping many people to better understand themselves and their place in the world, but that is not an objective feature of Shakespeare's words nor an objective property of the act of reading them. It is a property that emerged from a learner engaging their attention with the world evoked by Shakespeare's words so intently that the automatic, unconscious, and impossible to avoid process of learning then assimilated the meaning of those symbols (that simulated world) into its cognitive mapping process and thereby enabled that individual to gain a new perspective on their life and the world.

So from the education-as-attitude perspective, both the third (only experts determine what's educational) and fourth (enforced schooling is necessary to educate everyone) assumptions about learning and the state's interest in it must be rejected. The third assumption is based on the premise that what is "educational" is not simple and obvious; thus we need experts to objectively determine what kinds of materials and

Causal Storylines for Education	
Academics 1st Delivery	Attitude 1st Mapping
1- Shakespeare, Confucius, etc. write great books	
2- Readers read the great books	
3a- Readers pass the test	3b- Enthusiastic readers engage with the author's simulated reality so deeply that it alters the reader's maps (regardless of whether or not they pass a test) 3c- Bored readers engage with the author's composition only deeply enough to memorize enough content to pass a test 3d- Traumatized readers forget they read the book
4a- Readers are educated	4b- Enthusiastic readers are educated 4c- Bored readers remain ignorant 4d- Traumatized readers remain ignorant

activities are universally "educational." I concede that becoming successful in our complex society today is not simple and obvious, but it is also not possible to objectively determine what will or will not be "educational" before you have a specific student to educate. Boredom and trauma are not appropriate states of mind for instruction to be effective. The critical prerequisite to that student learning deeply is being in an open state of mind, which is commonly known as being enthusiastic or joyful. The assumption that experts are needed to objectively define certain materials or activities as universally "educational" is false.

The foundation of the fourth assumption is that the government can both know what is "educational" and then force children to have those materials or do those activities. Having rejected the possibility of there being universally "educational" materials or activities, then the fourth assumption must, naturally, be rejected as well.

Returning to the illiterate students who failed to learn to read and write despite being taught, we can take the parallel with the "blind-sight" phenomena a step further. In the same way that an accident or disease destroyed a portion of the brain of patients with "blind-sight," students who fail to learn the symbol manipulation behaviors taught in academics-first classrooms may have had their motivation to engage with those tools destroyed. A typical academics-first classroom uses a behavioral management power structure that ignores students' personal interests and concerns. In such a classroom, the exclusive measure of value is the exchange of manipulated symbols with no attention paid to student engagement. With little or no engagement, it is no surprise that some students not only fail to learn to read and write, but also fall into a pattern of consciousness that negates their motivation to engage with symbol manipulation activities. In short, they have fallen victim to motivational deficiencies with regard to literacy skills. The hapless teachers that attempt to "educate" children within coercive "academic" classrooms become inadvertently transformed into vectors of psychological negligence. This negligence arises from the relentless association of symbol manipulation activities with subjugation within power structures that minimize or ignore the children's primary psychological needs.[50]

Now we have to consider how to rectify our society's school system with the facts that 1) truly educational experiences depend on the degree of engagement that a child has with their activities, and 2) the state has a vested interest in ensuring that children achieve a truly educational level of deep connection with those activities.

---

[50] With just as much honesty and truthfulness we can repeat the same two sentences substituting the words "teacher" for "student" and "principal" (or other higher-ups) for "teacher." Subjugation within power structures that minimize or ignore human needs is always problematic.

The State's Interest Reconsidered

First of all, experts can help us. They can help identify the necessary qualities of different communities that have successfully facilitated deep engagement. Here are what I think are the twenty most relevant books in this area, in no particular order:

- *Streetlights and Shadows: Searching for the Keys to Adaptive Decision Making* by Gary Klein
- *The Unschooled Mind* by Howard Gardner
- *Assessing What Really Matters in Schools* by Ronald J. Newell & Mark J. Van Ryzin
- *Teach Like Finland* by Timothy D. Walker
- *In Search of Deeper Learning* by Jal Mehta & Sarah Fine
- *Make Me!* by Eric Toshalis
- *Professional Capital: Transforming Teaching in Every School* by Andy Hargeaves & Michael Fullan
- *For White Folks Who Teach In The Hood… and the Rest of Y'all Too: Reality Pedagogy and Urban Education* by Christopher Emdin
- *Intrinsic Motivation At Work* by Kenneth W. Thomas
- *The Power Of Full Engagement* by Jim Loehr & Tony Schwartz
- *The End of Average* by Todd Rose
- *Flow* by Milhaly Csikszentmihali
- *Deeper Learning: Beyond 21st Century Skills* Edited by James A. Bellanca
- *Deep Learning* by Michael Fullan, Joanne Quinn, & Joanne J. McEachen
- *Trusting Teachers With School Success* by Kim Farris-Berg & Edward J. Dirkswager
- *Deeper Learning* by Monica R. Martinez & Dennis McGrath
- *Rethinking Readiness* by Rafael Heller, Rebecca E. Wolfe, & Adria Steinberg
- *Anytime, Anywhere: Student-Centered Learning for Schools and Teachers* by Rebecca E. Wolfe, Nancy Hoffman, & Adria Steinberg

- *Wildflowers: A School Superintendent's Challenge to America* by Jonathan P. Raymond
- *Sources of Power: How People Make Decisions* by Gary Klein

The relevant experts are not those who evaluate materials and activities; the relevant experts are those who evaluate the qualities of communities and people's experiences in them. These kinds of experts will not analyze the materials and activities individuals happen to utilize in their educational process but instead will analyze the power structures, exchange processes, and patterns of consciousness that individuals experience in school communities. Second, we need to make the options between different power structures, exchange processes, and patterns of consciousness prominent in the minds of the general public (more prominent than competing reading programs like phonics and whole language).

I propose the 3R's of respect, responsibility, and resourcefulness as replacement assumptions around which we can organize our education systems:[51]

1. The State has an interest in promoting experiences for children in which the children choose to be a member of a group that treats them with respect, holds them responsible for the consequences of their actions, and encourages them to be resourceful in meeting their needs and the needs of others.

2. The full influence of government should be used to ensure that every child has the information, the ability, and the opportunity to choose to be a member of one or more groups that treat them with respect, hold them responsible, and encourage resourcefulness.

Notice that there is a distinction between "the State" which is a specific instance of governance and "the government" which is a general reference to the fact that groups of people always find ways to govern each other's behavior, even if they don't realize that they have done so.

---

[51] In my book *Education Can ONLY Be Offered: How K-12 Schools Will Save Democracy* (Berg, 2017) I explain these 3R's in more detail. The 3R's of virtue are the prerequisites to deeply learning the 3R's of academics.

The government includes families and all other means we use to govern each other's behavior. It is critically important to ensure that the State is not given charge of a task for which its coercive power is inappropriate. The daily behavior of children is not going to be well governed by the law enforcement mechanisms of the State. Different forms of governance are more appropriate for children. To give the government more specific guidance on how to discern groups that succeed from those that fail in their charge to teach these new 3R's (via their power structures, exchange processes, and patterns of consciousness) they could assess the patterns of need support, need satisfaction, motivation, and engagement of members of the group as indicators of the psychological climate of the organization under consideration.

We often assume that going to school is the key to future success. But this is true only if the child chooses to be engaged at the school they happen to end up in and if the school is an organization that treats them with respect, holds them responsible, and encourages them to be resourceful. Learning all the particular knowledge, skills, and information that they will need to become successful in today's complex world is going to require children to be deliberate, apply effort, and choose to engage with their experiences, not just go to school. Our job, as members of a state with a substantial vested interest in ensuring that children have better experiences, is to shape our communities to be the kinds of places where the power structures invite participation, the exchange processes are fair,[52] and the patterns of consciousness that result are usually positive. These are the kinds of communities in which people are deeply engaged with their experiences and make lasting contributions to their own lives, the lives of their families, their communities and, also, to the State. This line of thought has led me to believe that school leaders must teacher governance before academics, the first component of the Back to Basics 2.0 set of strategies.

Those headlines from the beginning of the chapter, about imprisoned parents, the shutdown of a democratic school, and children snatched away by various States, are the extreme, but logical, manifestations of

---

[52] Or at least have the capability of becoming more fair when the members of the community engage with their collective decision-making processes.

erroneous assumptions about what is "educational" and how the state should act on its interest in education. The current assumptions that the state makes as it regulates how schools and families facilitate education only make sense from an outdated and mistaken perspective. It is time to challenge and reformulate those assumptions to reflect what is currently known about learning. The individual's need to be educated can be aligned with the state's obligation to cultivate an educated citizenry. Education policy needs to be shaped by a more accurate understanding of education itself. I call this an attitude-first perspective on learning; applying state influence to achieve it will help ensure that all organizations that serve children achieve the deeper learning necessary for good citizenship.

Once there is an opening for robust dialogue about how human needs are being supported, it will be important to ensure that systemic changes do not inadvertently replicate the inequities that are already in place. In the next chapter I share the results of a thought experiment which takes our transportation system to be reasonably equitable and uses it as a model to suggest ways that our education system could become more so. By considering the properties of the transportation system as the best available model of equity on a large scale I constructed what should be plausible design criteria for education.

3 ITERATING TOWARD SYSTEMATIC EQUITY IN SCHOOLS

Creating equity is the most important challenge that our system faces. We are failing both ourselves and our posterity as long as we perpetuate a system that maintains so much ignorance and misery amidst so much wealth. While we have achieved a great deal to be proud of, it would be disingenuous for us to rest on our laurels.

Our transportation system is probably the single most equitable institution in our society today. It does not pass muster in every way, but it strikes me as the one large-scale system that appears to most fully meet the criteria. Think about how comprehensive our transportation system is. Just about anyone can get just about anywhere. The tools and systems for transportation span the gamut from shoes to bicycles to cars to jet airplanes. We empower just about everyone to self-determine their location without directly controlling them. We have a variety of ways to encourage them to make choices, both wise and unwise, with some thought to making the most common unwise choices minimally disruptive. For instance, we give people the freedom to neglect the maintenance of their cars up to the point at which they cause harm to someone else. A recent case in point occurred here in Oregon when a driver killed a bicyclist. "Deputy District Attorney Elisabeth Waner said Schrantz [the driver] knew the tires of his Toyota 4Runner had lost nearly all of their tread and were causing the pickup truck to fishtail and slide around corners in wet weather, yet he continued driving."[53] The driver pleaded guilty to criminally negligent homicide and received a sentence of three and a half years in jail for not properly maintaining his truck. While we put some reasonable restrictions on the means of transporting ourselves and our stuff, we don't presume to know where each person should go nor which means they should use to get where they want to be.

We may feel completely unrestrained in the moment when we are transporting ourselves from one place to another, but that is an illusion. There are myriad constraints of which we are simply unaware in that moment. Having that sense of being unrestrained should be a reasonable expectation for everyone in an equitable system (not in every moment, but in general). I may feel constrained by the slow traffic that I encounter on the freeway during my commute, but that is not a sign of inequity, it is a sign of an inconvenience caused by transportation infrastructure and systems designs that are being challenged by unprecedented population growth here in the Portland area. As long as the larger system is operating in an equitable way then some combination of adaptations of the transportation system and societal expectations will allow me to continue to achieve my goals, even if I have to put up with some inconvenience in the process.

Now, consider airports. There are lots of ways to build airports, and I don't know how y'all would build one in your particular community. I have no way of knowing what your transportation infrastructure already has in place and what your airport would need to fit into that context. But I can be confident that it will meet some design principles that would make it fit into the transportation system more broadly.

If public airports were regulated like mainstream K-12 public schools are currently, then everyone would be required to have travel agents who control where you go and how you get there. You would have new travel agents every year and in the latter part of the process the number of travel agents would expand from one or two in the elementary years to seven or more in high school. Universal standardization would be an obvious

---

53 URL: https://goo.gl/cXWwKP (OregonLive.com)

solution to the complexity of handling so many imposed itineraries. A massive bureaucratic and political nightmare would be the result, which happens to reflect current reality in our mainstream K-12 education system, but not our transportation system.

The following table uses the airport analogy as a thought experiment to understand how deeper learning schools within our education ecology should have certain similarities to airports within the transportation ecology. The left column takes the airport/ transportation side and the right column presents a parallel construction for school/ education. The italics indicate the substantive changes between the two columns.

Transportation vs. Education Table

Transportation System	*Education* System
Guiding question	
How do *airports* (and the *transportation* system, more broadly) succeed at facilitating the *mobility* of multitudes of *people* every day without directly controlling their activities?	How do *schools* (and *could* the *education* system, more broadly) succeed at facilitating the *education* of multitudes of *children* every day without directly controlling their activities?

Units of analysis	
Travelers (people traveling)	*Learners* (people learning)
Travel Catalysts (*airport* service providers such as *airlines, cab companies, restaurants, travel agents,* etc.)	*Learning* Catalysts (*school* service providers such as *teachers, food services, disability specialists,* etc.)
Travel Context (e.g. *airports, cities, government regulations, flying technologies,* etc.)	*Learning* Context (e.g. *schools, cities, tutoring services, camps, after school programs, books,* etc.)
Design Principles	
Travelers make their own decisions.	*Learners* make their own decisions *(within the contexts of their families and communities).*
Travel Catalysts serve *travelers.*	*Learning* Catalysts serve *learners.*
The *Travel* Context is designed to make the relationship between *travelers* and their chosen catalysts as easy as possible given certain minimum standards of health, safety, and fairness.	The *Learning* Context is designed to make the relationship between *learners* and their chosen catalysts as easy as possible given certain minimum standards of health, safety, and fairness *(including provisions for primary human need support).*

Only the *traveler* is responsible for ensuring that they each have a *destination* and deciding how they should *get to their destination*.	Only the *learner* is responsible for ensuring they have a *goal* and deciding how they should *pursue their goal*. *(Keep in mind that all humans have some unconscious goals derived from their primary human needs and that children are assumed to be inescapably embedded in and influenced by their family and the wider community.)*
The *travel* industry is made up of interlocking sets of organizations of people responsible for making sure that *travelers* have catalysts available to help them.	The *education* industry is made up of interlocking sets of organizations of people responsible for making sure that *learners* have catalysts available to help them. *(Ideally the education industry and its component organizations represent well-structured communities, an idea discussed in more detail below this table.)*

The *port authority is* the organization of people responsible for ensuring that each *airport* is organized appropriately to facilitate the relationships between *travelers* and their chosen catalysts.	The *administrations of schools, districts, state/federal education agencies, charter granting agencies, or education management organizations are* the organizations of people responsible for ensuring that each *school* is organized appropriately to facilitate the relationships between *learners* and their chosen catalysts.
Airport management knows that the most important outcome is ensuring that all the *travelers* who choose to *fly into and/or out of that airport* have the ability to find their way through the system in pursuit of their own goals.	*School* management knows that the most important outcome is ensuring that all the *learners* who choose to *attend that school* have the ability to find their way through the system in pursuit of their own goals.
Each service provider within the *airport* is presumed to be an expert on what they do to further the *travelers'* goals.	Each service provider *(teacher or other activity facilitator)* within the *school* is presumed to be an expert on what they do to further the *learners'* goals.

Enabling *travelers* to achieve their goals is the primary gauge of success for service providers (via autonomous choices within a regulated service provider market).	Enabling the *learners* to achieve their goals is the primary gauge of success for service providers (via autonomous choices within a regulated service provider market. *A market in the sense that children have meaningful choices for pursuing their goals and aspirations, not in a financial sense*).
The service providers rely on the *airport* to enable them to communicate with *travelers* in a variety of ways so that the *travelers* can make good decisions *(via signage and other forms of information distribution.)*	The service providers rely on the *school* to enable them to communicate with *learners* in a variety of ways so that the *learners* can make good decisions *(via newsletters, course catalogs, etc.)*
The service providers also enable the *travelers* to adjust their decisions on the fly as either the situation changes or they discover that they have made a mistake.	The service providers also enable the *learners* to adjust their decisions on the fly as either the situation changes or they discover that they have made a mistake.

All children and adults need access to a community support system that nurtures them, as nurturing is defined in the resolution in Chapter 7. Schools should be designed to provide that (with outside help, as needed). Too many children do not have equitable access to such a system. The effectiveness of adults charged with nurturing responsibilities should be evaluated in light of data on the well-being, motivation, and engagement of their students. Adults cannot know whether or not they have met their moral obligations if they do not have reasonably objective information about those psychological aspects of their students' experiences. The design criteria in the table above can serve as a principled guide to where we want to end up, with a well-structured education system.

Well-structured communities are the key to sustainable success. In well-structured communities, mistakes are accepted as a normal part of being in community for both adults and children. Well-structured communities continue to function no matter who makes a mistake. Mistakes are taken as opportunities to be more supportive, not less. Communities can be well-structured both within their organizational boundaries and as part of the overlapping sets of organizations that make up the industry. Education includes families, schools, businesses, government agencies, and civil society (NGO's/non-profits). Well-structured communities will have a multitude of individuals and organizations serving critical functions across the spectrum of possibilities to ensure that there will be support provided even if some of the individuals or organizations fail or make mistakes.

Equitable access to educational opportunities and resources is important. Equitable access would be one of the key criteria for discerning the quality of the structure of a community. Judgements of whether access is absent or inequitably present should start with an analysis of how well supported primary human needs are across the population before other considerations are included. For instance, the disparities in scores on standardized tests that appear to be based on race or any other oppression indicator are not currently solvable equity issues because of the pervasive lack of need support for the children who are subjected to the tests. The organizations representing traditionally oppressed populations that have called for compliance with the testing mandates are well-intentioned but mistaken in their support for compliance. The central equity issue they should be focused on is access to primary human need support in schools, not academic support. Primary need support improves academic outcomes so this is a matter of getting both/and not either/or.

Another example of an equity issue being misunderstood is standards. Standards are great, but only for those who choose to meet them. We do not make everyone become a doctor, but when someone chooses to become a doctor then they are simultaneously choosing to meet professional standards. Imposing standards universally should be carefully reserved for instances that have the potential for tragedy such as: the structural safety of bridges and buildings, public health measures for controlling communicable diseases, and supporting primary human needs. Enforcing universal academic standards on children is *not* necessary. But enforcing universal standards for supporting primary human needs in schools may be essential.

The key "on the ground" behavioral change is to spread the use of need supportive management techniques instead of need thwarting or need neglecting techniques (which are now understood to be intolerable expedients). The key "10,000 foot" or high level change is to create policies that discourage or punish primary need thwarting management and encourage or enforce primary need supportive management.

Changing organizations is not easy and it would be counterproductive for me or anyone else to summarily dictate a universal solution. Instead, I am providing design criteria and suggesting ways of structuring the different discussions you can have for addressing the challenges you face in your particular school, agency, or community. This process of rethinking the project is a necessary preliminary step before undertaking a design process, because using the same mental model as before would reproduce the same problematic patterns that got us into trouble in the first place due to the nature of the hidden curriculum (as presented in the next chapter)).

4 A PSYCHOLOGICAL PERSPECTIVE ON HUMAN NATURE

Recall Back to Basics version 2.0 that I called for at the end of Chapter 1. Before I can help you fully make sense of Basics 2.0 and deeper learning I need to share with you a deeper insight into my perspective. I take it as a given, based on my extensive study of psychology, that there are aspects of the realities of education, schooling, and learning that are hidden from us. This is not an assumption that most people make, but should. Over the next two chapters I am going to reveal what I have learned about the relationship between K-12 schooling and psychology and how those insights change everything we understand about education.

The Disconnect

There is a deep disconnect between K-12 schooling and psychology. This is despite the fact that the media presents to educators a constant stream of books and articles that share research findings about brains, neurological functions, and our tendencies toward irrational behaviors. The disconnect between schooling and psychology is "deep," not because educators are behind on research findings, which is true but unremarkable; it is because they have not yet come to realize that psychologists are changing their view of human nature. What the educators, the education media, and the policy makers who manage our

K-12 school system have not yet picked up on is the emerging shift in psychologists' fundamental conception of what a human being is and what that means for education. Until educators grasp the psychologists' insights into human nature, they will not be able to draw useful lessons from the research.

There has been high profile coverage of psychologist Walter Mischel's famous line of research into willpower from the 1970's, popularly known as the Marshmallow Test. The Marshmallow Test is an experimental design in which children, usually three and four years old, are brought into a room equipped with only a table and chair for the child and a two-way mirror for the experimenters (see the photo montage below). The child is not made aware that the mirror allows the experimenters to observe them. After establishing trust with the child through other activities, the experimenter proposes a "game" in which the child is offered a marshmallow. If the child would like to have two marshmallows then s/he must refrain from eating the marshmallow left in front of them on a plate while the experimenter leaves the child alone in the room for a length of time of which the child is not aware. The experimental variations have included using things other than marshmallows that were established as desirable items for the children. The "rewards" have even included abstract tokens that would be exchanged for more tangible items. The children's perception of the trustworthiness of the experimenters was varied in some recent

The Marshmallow Test

replications, though the early experimenters claim to have taken that variable into account in their original design. Other variations included giving the children different kinds of hints about how to cope.

Walter Mischel's work, beyond just the Marshmallow Test, has been especially instrumental in transforming how psychologists conceptualize the person, as demonstrated by a) the publication of a whole volume of research inspired by his work, b) how it has informed various aspects of psychology, and c) how it represents a paradigm shift in the field.[54]

Mischel's main finding from the Marshmallow Test would *seem* to be that young children who exhibit more self-control will fare better in later life than those who exhibit less. A *New York Times* reporter summed up the usual conclusion as "Character is destiny."[55] However, according to a recent peer-reviewed study surveying this line of work, "many academic and popular renditions of the lessons to be learned from this program of research run counter to the conceptual intent, empirical findings, and explicitly stated precautions of the published research."[56] The lessons that educators should draw from Mischel's research are not about cultivating children's skill at deploying willpower nor about their character traits; they are about embedding children in an environment, observing the ways various relationships between the children and the environment produce different patterns of interaction, and then adjusting the environment to achieve more productive interactions (which may include building skills and developing traits). But drawing those lessons out of the research requires a conception of being human that goes beyond describing children in terms of their individual skills and traits. The descriptions need to emphasize the relationships and interactions that influence what skills and traits the children exhibit.

This is like a figure-to-background shift, as in the perceptual task of being able to discern a person or object in the foreground of a drawing or photo and then changing your focus to concentrate on how the background indicates the situation in which the figure exists. This type

---

[54] Shoda, Cervone & Downey, 2007 (See References for full citations.)

[55] Bourne, 2014

[56] Peake, 2017

Famous Bistable Images

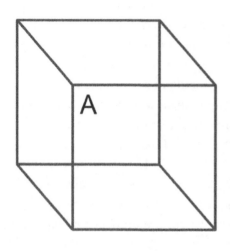

Corner A: in front or behind?   Vase or Profiles?

Necker Cube   Silver Jubilee Vase

of shift is best illustrated with a certain kind of visual illusion called a bi-stable image. Two famous examples of these illusions are shown above. The Necker cube presents us with a two-dimensional drawing that our brains automatically interpret as a three-dimensional object in which the corner labelled 'A' can be either projecting out to the front of the cube or settled into the back. The Silver Jubilee vase is a foreground object and then when you shift your focus to the background it enables you to see that the sides are shaped to present the profiles of Prince Philip and Queen Elizabeth.[57]

According to a line of research led by psychologist Richard Nisbett, in most Western European (individualist) cultures there is a default tendency to focus primarily on the figure, whereas in most East Asian (collectivist) cultures the default tends to take the background more into

---

[57] The vase is the subject of this 2 minute video:
https://www.youtube.com/watch?v=neVhYZ1XWFY.

account.[58] Those experiments used pictures such as the one below of fish in a tank.

It's an unremarkable illustration, but it turns out that your cultural background determines how likely you are to focus on the properties of the fish the experimenters ask you to look at versus how much is known about the fish based on the background information that surrounds it. Despite the fact that there is a tendency to privilege either the figure or the situational embeddedness of the figure portrayed, a full and complete understanding of the depiction requires both. Any choice of emphasis should be determined by a combination of the contextual factors of the situation in which the perceiver is embedded and the goals the perceiver has in that situation. The optimal solution to the problem of whether to focus on the figure versus the background, in situations that are more complex than merely looking at fish, should hinge on which will provide you with the information you need to get what you want from the situation. If you do not have the cognitive flexibility to adjust your perceptual behavior to the requirements of the situation (no matter what

---

[58] Nisbett, 2007

default emphasis your culture may provide you with), then you run the risk of failing to get what you want.

Which is more important in determining human behavior: individual disposition/ personality/ character or the situation in which the individual is embedded? This has been a perennial debate in psychology, but the fact is that both are necessary.[59] Consider the possibility that the disposition vs. situation debate is like a bi-stable image. The fact is that the alternative interpretation is always present, but it is difficult, maybe even impossible, to hold both interpretations in place simultaneously. If we want to respond accurately and appropriately then we need to cultivate the cognitive flexibility that is required to move smoothly between the alternative interpretations. In the long term we will succeed at adjusting to the ever-changing requirements of our situations to the degree that we reinforce a cognitive flexibility that would lead us to use both interpretations, as needed.

Psychology: The Mind Science

The field of psychology has nominally concerned itself with how we exist as individual minds. In the early 1990's psychiatrist Daniel J. Siegel thought it odd that the field had not arrived at a definition of the term "mind."[60] So, he sought a consensus definition from a group of over 40 experts concerned with the relationship between the mind and the brain, from anthropologists to neuroscientists. They all agreed that the mind is an embodied and relational process that monitors and modifies flows of energy and information.

The feature of the mind that is the most prominent in our day-to-day experience is the self. The neuroscientist Antonio Damasio makes a persuasive case for the self having three different functional aspects related to how brains generate certain types of experiences: the protoself, the core self, and the extended self.[61] The protoself is a feature of all animals with brains. It is a neural mapping of the organism's body that

---

[59] Deci & Ryan, 1980

[60] Siegel, 2012

[61] Damasio, 2010

produces what Damasio calls "primordial feeling." This is a primitive feature of sensation that allows us to be awake and attuned to the most basic aspects of being alive.

The core self adds to the protoself a mapping of the self in relation to an object or, more broadly, the world of objects. The core self gives us a sense of a now moment which spans a small amount of time (up to the scale of minutes). This now provides us with a whole suite of capabilities for interacting with the world in reference to what we have non-consciously learned about how the world works and how we can get what we want from it.

The extended self is the bit that might be a uniquely human aspect of the mind. The extended self is an imaginative system for creating multiple versions of the self in relation to the environment, enabling us to vary our concepts about the past and future. Unlike other primates who seem to be trapped in the present, our extended self allows us to have the sense that we are living out a whole lifetime that we can plan for and remember in ways that other animals do not. Thanks to the ways language and some cultures extend our concepts of ourselves into collective identities, some of us also develop a sense of history that transcends our individual lived experiences.

Psychologist Daniel Gilbert describes the human mind as an experience simulator. [62] Thanks to that particular feature of our neural hardware, we have the ability to internally simulate both the consequences of intended courses of future action and imagine what *could have* occurred in the past, not just remember what *did* happen. Human learning is fundamentally about growing these mental maps of ourselves, the environment in which we are embedded, and the relationship between them so that we can respond appropriately across spans of time and space unequalled by any other animal.

The focus on "individual minds" above is a matter of narrative convention. Encouraged by this convention and, perhaps, the individualism of Western culture, we like to think that our dispositions, character traits, or personalities (our basic units or sources of

---

[62] Gilbert, 2006

personhood) are the primary causal factors that determine our behavior. This bias towards attributing our behavior to internal properties of ourselves is the basis for encouraging educators to train children to use their "willpower" or to develop more desirable character traits that can overcome their "impulsivity." It is reinforced under the influence of the typical interpretation of the Marshmallow Test, or perhaps that bias is the source of those misinterpretations. However, the field of psychology does not confine itself to this kind of "individual." What is traditionally regarded as an individual mind represents only a small proportion of the concerns of the field. While there is a great deal of important knowledge organized around understanding the psychological "self," much of the field has conceded that the social and cultural situations in which individuals are embedded and the biological situations out of which they are embodied have much more influence on individual behavior than is normally supposed.[63] The psychological "self," or individual mind, is but one of many determining factors in human behavior.

The notion that the "I" that I experience as causing my behavior is somehow at the mercy of the universe does not sit well with the usual intuitive notions about what most of us take our "self" to be. Despite the diversity of causes of psychological content within our minds, we each experience a remarkably consistent continuity of selfhood which appears to be at odds with the notion that our behavior is mostly caused by that vast array of forces that are either internally non-conscious or externally imperceptible. Because of that tension, the debate about the relative contributions of individual dispositions versus the situational context has been a staple in the field for decades. The question is whether your behavior is caused by your internal characteristics/ personality/ dispositions versus by the situational factors or circumstances in which you are embedded. It is similar to other scientific debates like the biological debate over nature versus nurture or the debate in physics about whether light is a wave versus a particle. In every one of these cases the answer is that both are necessary for understanding the phenomena in question.

---

[63] For explanations of the disposition vs. situation debate see Bower (2007); Hanson & Yosifon (2003, 2004).

The original terms of this kind of debate are ultimately unresolvable; and to understand why consider a debate among ancient geometers about the creation of squareness. Imagine that one school of thought originally set out to argue that the vertical sides are *more* important than the horizontal ones while a competing school of thought decided to argue the opposite. Because of the propositional logic that now characterizes geometry, in which squareness is clearly *defined* by the presence of both vertical and horizontal sides, it is simply absurd to *debate* their relative contributions. While each side in these kinds of debates were in a certain sense "correct" to assert the importance of their favored aspect of the reality in question, it is only when the inescapable necessity of *both* sides are accepted that a proper understanding can arise. The original terms of the debate must be abandoned, or more accurately, transcended. The solution is to formulate a unified conception that establishes the interrelationship between the previously opposed sides.

The fact is that the psychological self, an individual mind, is one among an impressive array of contextual factors that determine human behavior, both internally and externally. It is *both* situation *and* disposition that determine our behavior. Our uniquely personal perceptions, thoughts, actions, goals, aspirations, and even our understanding of our context are largely caused by the alignment of a vast array of phenomena that occur entirely outside of what we each experience as our "self." And yet it is usually this "self" which is naïvely taken to be the proper subject of the field of psychology.

The most famous and dramatic examples of research that demonstrate the surprising power of situational influences on human behavior are the Obedience To Authority studies led by Stanley Milgram[64] and the Stanford Prison Experiment led by Philip Zimbardo.[65] This body of research was originally intended to figure out how "authorities" influence the behavior of people in subservient positions to them. It was inspired by the revelation of atrocities during World War II. Responsibility for those atrocities was (and is) often attributed to the

---

[64] Historical review by Russell, 2011

[65] Zimbardo, 2013

"evil" intentions of individual people (e.g. Adolph Hitler), where it is assumed that the "evil" is a property of an individual's mind. Psychologists decided to test that assumption. Throughout this body of research a shockingly high proportion of otherwise normal and mentally healthy people (meaning not "evil") participated in causing innocent people to experience extreme pain and suffering (though in Milgram's studies it was only a simulation, not the real thing, which experimental subjects only found out afterwards). The experiments were designed to ensure that any variations in the character or dispositions of individuals were either excluded from the beginning or would cancel each other out across a population. The point of the many experiments described in this literature was to ensure that the causes of the observed behaviors could be correctly and logically attributed. After decades of research the conclusion is that your situation causes much more of your behavior than you would ever realize just from your intuition. Despite your sense that your "self" is usually the cause of your behavior, you are wrong. To be fair, I completely share in that sense and I am just as wrong about it as you are, and the same goes for all psychologists.

If situations are so powerful, then how do psychologists reconcile our intuitions about the causal efficacy of our "selves" with their scientific findings? Should we conclude that the "self" is merely an illusion, like the dimension of depth we falsely see in the 2-D Necker cube from page 66, or a fantasy, like the Easter Bunny shown on the right? Let's take a broader view for a moment and also consider some issues of schooling before we address these questions.

Easter Bunny

Human Nature

Through a variety of scientific and mathematical explorations that extend well beyond psychology, we are confident that all humans live within epistemic horizons that make all possible mappings of ourselves, the situations in which we exist, and their relations incomplete. [66] An epistemic horizon is like the event horizon of a black hole. The event horizon is a boundary beyond which light cannot escape. It forms a bubble of gravitational influence with the black hole situated at the center. An epistemic horizon is a limit beyond which our understanding does not extend. Think of that boundary as forming a bubble that limits what understandings the person at the center can apply to the experiences that they have. The individual is looking out from the center, but the epistemic bubble that surrounds them means that they have limited access to the full reality in which they and their bubble are embedded.

Simon-Pierre Laplace famously speculated that an imaginary demon could in principle, by knowing the position and momentum of every particle in the universe, know the indefinite future and past. He was wrong. With regard to complex adaptive systems, such as organisms, organizations, societies, and ecologies, we cannot know to any significant degree of certainty, even in principle, the past or the future beyond a short window of time. The suite of insights that contribute to this humbling conclusion includes:

- Heisenberg's uncertainty principle in physics
- Gödel's incompleteness theorem in mathematics
- the unpredictability of completely deterministic and relatively simple iterative mathematical equations discovered by Gaston Julia and further developed by Benoit Mandelbrot
- Poincaré's discovery that complex systems are so extraordinarily sensitive to initial conditions that they are effectively unpredictable (popularized later by Edward Lorentz as the Butterfly Effect)

---

[66] Williamson, 2016

- from cartography the aphorism that says, "The only complete map of the world *is the world.*"

These insights lead to the conclusion that no one individual can ever achieve a complete understanding of themselves nor their context, which means we can never achieve objectively perfect perception, thought, action, nor even goals and aspirations. There is uncertainty and that uncertainty is forever inherent to our existence, regardless of whether we realize it or not. Our individual epistemic horizons are small and will always be small relative to the universe, no matter how cleverly we enlarge them, either individually or collectively.

While we cannot ever have complete knowledge of the universe, that does not prevent us from having enough information and understanding to achieve some of our specific purposes. We have already come up with some amazing enlargements of our epistemic horizons that have enabled us to create the complex technological society in which we find ourselves living today. While we cannot ultimately overcome our epistemic horizons, we **can** overcome the limitations of our knowledge of how to achieve many specific goals and aspirations. There may be no way to know which limitations are within the realm of being overcome or not, so there is good reason to approach most challenges with great hope for success.[67]

Our current mainstream school system was designed to act as if the universe is knowable and that the conscious psychological self, *without* considering the situation in which it is embedded, is the right object of analysis for understanding education and the learning process at the heart of that enterprise. For example, laws and policies here in the USA routinely require every single child in every class to be individually tested and graded in order to measure outcomes, without the slightest regard for the variations across classrooms, schools, cities, counties, and states. There is an assumption that each individual student is just another atom in the assembly of social molecules that make up a societal machine or

---

[67] For an extended exploration of scientific limitations see du Sautoy (2016) and for a combination of cognitive linguistic and philosophical analysis of how we know what we know see Lakoff & Johnson (1999)

organism, depending on your favored metaphor. Attempting to understand the individual as an indivisible "atomic" unit that stands in a privileged position in our analyses is like attempting to understand physics using Aristotle's "essential elements" of air, water, fire, and earth. In all the material sciences, and all the fields of engineering related to them, there is no longer any meaningful application for that set of concepts. Even the original concept of the "atom" has been abandoned because there is no longer any scientific use for the idea that there is a single indivisible level of material stuff in the universe. In this same way, the field of psychology does not use the term "self" in the way it was originally meant. There is no indivisible psychological structure, process, nor even pattern that can be unambiguously labeled a "self." For convenience I will refer to this outmoded notion of the self as an "atomic self."

The term "self" is still useful when we refer to certain aggregations of structures, processes, and patterns, as in Damasio's work, but there is not a single unchanging entity to which it refers. Philosopher Daniel Dennett has posited that the self is like the center of gravity of a physical object.[68] The physical center of gravity of a hoop, for instance, is neither an illusion nor a fantasy even though it is located mathematically and invisibly in thin air. It is a useful conceptual tool that is fictional, but not fantastical. Dennett proposed that we should think of the self as a *narrative* center of gravity. It is an extremely useful fiction for making predictions.

Behaviorist theory is predicated on the idea that behaviors that are reinforced will increase in frequency. Yet, when researchers reinforce behaviors that children do spontaneously without reinforcement (such as drawing) then the result is a decrease in the behavior rather than the

---

[68] Dennett, 1992

75

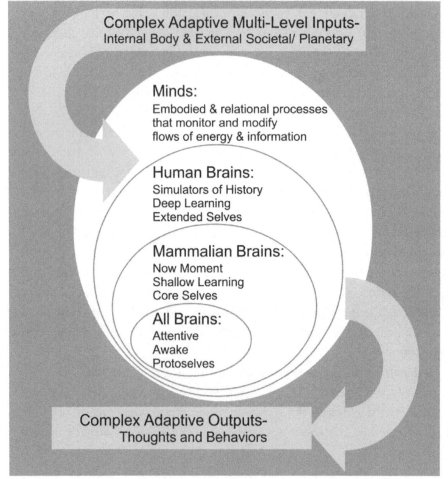

Views of
the Self

Knowable Universe

Consciously Guided
Character-driven
Atomic Selves

vs.

Complex Adaptive Multi-Level Inputs-
Internal Body & External Societal/ Planetary

Minds:
Embodied & relational processes
that monitor and modify
flows of energy & information

Human Brains:
Simulators of History
Deep Learning
Extended Selves

Mammalian Brains:
Now Moment
Shallow Learning
Core Selves

All Brains:
Attentive
Awake
Protoselves

Complex Adaptive Outputs-
Thoughts and Behaviors

predicted increase. Self-Determination Theory arose in the 1970's in the context of this observation. By positing a "self" that attends to whether the volitional and causal sources of its own activities are more internal rather than external, it is possible to make more accurate predictions about the children's behavior. The decrease in the target behavior is explained by the fact that the child understands that the use of "rewards" indicates that the child is being manipulated by an outside force; therefore the activity is not as desirable as one that is more internally generated. The behavioral principle remains true, but in order to accurately anticipate many human behaviors, a "self" that modifies what counts as reinforcement is necessary. Reinforcement contingencies are modified according to how the "self" perceives the satisfaction or thwarting of primary needs.

We make categorical errors if we look for the self in a specific location in the body, presume it has specific knowable boundaries, or expect that a teacher can reliably manipulate its traits. Not being physically "real" does not diminish how useful it is when applied to appropriate problems, but we need to be careful about our understanding and use of the concept.[69]

The Views of the Self Diagram on the previous page illustrates how much more complex the emerging understanding of the self is compared to the more intuitive view that is more commonly held. Before moving

---

[69] Each of us humans consistently reports being, or having, a *self*. Our self seems to be a *singular* consistent entity across time and space. It also appears to be the conscious causal source of our behaviors and has a *continuity* across most of our experiences. These perceptions are explained by regularities and continuities across many different levels of reality that we don't normally associate with our selves. There are multiple reasons for the regularities and continuities we experience. The physical environment that we encounter everywhere on the planet has very consistent *underlying* properties even as the obviously perceptible properties we observe at many different locations can vary considerably. All humans are biologically built along very similar lines. The interactions between the consistent physical properties of the world and our very similar biological structures can be presumed to create highly consistent perceptual experiences. Philosophical conjectures to the contrary, there appear to be sufficient commonalities between our physiology and the reliability of the underlying physics that the red I see is the same red you do (though I am less certain that your pet dog, cat, bat, tarantula, lizard, or whatever sees the same red we do). There is some variation, as in colorblindness, but it is systematic and neatly explained with reference to the same scientific models. Certain of our needs as both individuals and a species are also highly consistent. And the relational, organizational, and societal situations we each encounter from day-to-day are highly similar most of the time. Despite our normally being unable to accurately detect the causal factors that generate our behavior, the consistency we experience as a self is not a delusion. It is based on actual regularities and consistencies, even if we usually do not have an accurate grasp of their causal sources.

Stand and Deliver

on to consider how these insights into psychology affect education I want to bring home the point about how limited the self is with regard to the situation in which it is embedded and out of which it is embodied. Assuming you are an educator or are at least familiar with the current educational zeitgeist, then you will be familiar with the phrase "hidden curriculum." The idea is easy to illustrate but difficult to understand unless you are up to date on the emerging notion of human nature coming out of psychology. All those inner city urban school movies I mentioned before in the introduction provide ample illustration.

Stand and Deliver is the dramatization of the year 1982 when Jaime Escalante had a class of 15 students in his AP calculus class and 14 of them passed the AP Calculus exam. Afterwards the Educational Testing Service, who administers the exam, did an analysis that suggested the students had cheated. Twelve of the students agreed to be retested and all twelve scored well enough to have their original scores reinstated. At the beginning of the movie there are a series of scenes that portray classroom and school chaos including students openly disregarding Escalante's instructions, making irrelevant public comments about sex education in math class, and a school yard fight. A few weeks later, in what is falsely portrayed as his first year of teaching, Escalante, in a staff meeting about threats to the school's accreditation and a shortage of funding, declares that he can teach advanced mathematics using only "ganas," translated as "desire," to get his students to succeed. He not only gets them to study in the basic math class he started the year with but got them all to study throughout a summer vacation including Saturdays in preparation for taking his AP Calculus class.

What they did not portray was that Escalante had been teaching for five years before proposing to teach a calculus class and that he had several years of teaching it before the fateful year in which his students were accused of cheating. What they could not portray was the fact that within a few years of the movie coming out he, and nearly all of his colleagues who made the program work, left the school and the program effectively collapsed.[70] His was indeed a heroic effort but the institutional reality of bureaucratic schooling in that district was not able to maintain the "ganas." The hidden curriculum was like a tide washing away his miraculous little sand castle.

Most of the fictionalized movies mentioned in the introduction, like *Stand and Deliver*, begin with a naïve teacher just starting out at the school in which they perform their miracle. The teachers and students that were already established in the school are portrayed as behaving in ways that everyone would agree are 1) undesirable and 2) not explicitly taught. In spite of the opinions, inclinations, thoughts, beliefs, and desires of those teachers and students, they tend to behave badly. What makes the stories of the featured "naïve" teachers and the students who ended up in their classes remarkable was that they were able to behave better despite the countervailing biological, relational, organizational, cultural, and societal forces that pushed them towards worse behavior. It is those forces that

Photo By Richard Sloane, Used with permission

make up the hidden curriculum.

Now, let me make it a little more personal by giving you a demonstration. I am about to give you two sets of instructions regarding the picture of my face to the left.

First instruction: after you are looking at my face, in any way

[70] See: http://reason.com/archives/2002/07/01/stand-and-deliver-revisited

you can, stop looking at my face. Easy, huh? All you had to do was close your eyes or look away.

Second instruction: after you are looking at my face, while you continue to look at my eyes, my cheeks, and my mouth, in any way you can stop seeing my nose. Give it the old college try. Not easy, is it? In fact, if you follow the directions to the letter, the task is literally impossible. Despite the fact that the set of instructions is logical, grammatically correct, and fully coherent, they are directing you to do something that you are incapable of accomplishing. Most people will not even notice that fact until after they have made the effort and failed at the task. We are not naturally able to foresee the impossibility of that task if we rely solely on the words of the instructions.

Let's pretend that you are charged with teaching a lesson about eyes, cheeks, and mouths, but not noses. If you are going to present those features to students in their natural context of a face, but do not take appropriate measures to ensure that the nose is not available to be seen, then the nose will be included in the lesson regardless of your intentions and the clarity of your directions. They will come along for the ride because normal human brains are wired to see a face as a whole experience. There is no way that the conscious experiencing self of a student can, at your command, cognitively edit out the nose from his/her perceptual experience of a face. If the nose is not supposed to be included in that lesson on the other features of the face, then you *must* remove the nose from the facial context by careful construction of the situation.

The lesson about facial features is silly, of course, but the point is that hidden curricula are subtle features of human experience. We can use proper grammar and logic to coherently construct instructional situations in which unintended and counterproductive features of the situation will intrude on the experiences of teachers and students despite everyone's best intentions. The hidden curricula that lead to bad behaviors and disengagement in schools are not going to be sustainably altered by the opinions, inclinations, thoughts, beliefs, and desires of individuals. However, I am advocating for the development of individual opinions, inclinations, thoughts, beliefs, and desires that are consistent with supporting primary human needs. But *sustained* positive change requires the organizational, cultural, and societal levels of power to be applied to the shaping of those opinions, inclinations, thoughts, beliefs, and desires.

Despite the possibility that the instructional imperatives of mainstream schools may be logical, grammatically correct, and coherent, it does not mean that they are asking teachers and students to do things of which they are inherently capable. Recall Back to Basics 2.0; if students and teachers are asked to learn deeply in the context of their primary human needs being thwarted or neglected, they are being asked to do something that is impossible. But, that impossibility is very difficult to discern, and we are all more likely to blame the students and teachers for not trying hard enough than we are to question the viability of the demands of the system (due to our current epistemic horizon bubbles).

We need to be resigned to the fact that there will always be a hidden curriculum. Hidden curricula are an inherent consequence of being embedded in and embodied by complex adaptive systems. But if we can align the different levels of the education system to support primary human needs, then we will cause deeper learning to be a more frequent occurrence and achieve sustainable positive change in schools. Achieving that kind of alignment will need to start with revisiting some of the most basic issues in education in light of what we have learned about ourselves. That is the topic of the next chapter.

Don Berg

5 THE PSYCHOLOGICAL FOUNDATIONS OF DEEPER LEARNING

What is an educated person?

In order to proceed let's be clear about how to conceive of an educated person. My conception is broader than most people's, I suspect. This conception is deliberately broad enough to transcend and include academic excellence. I take it as a baseline that an educated person is, literally,

> someone who perceives accurately, thinks clearly, and acts effectively on self-selected goals and aspirations that are appropriate to their situation, without explicitly knowing that those various things are going on.

These are processes that occur outside of awareness. Despite the illusion that we "know our own mind," the mental activities that determine our behavior are implicit, not explicit. Learning is the only process that can transform someone into an educated person. That process requires interactions between the person and the situation they are supposed to master, or an accurate simulation of it.[71] Those interactions enable the

---

[71] Klein, 1999 (See References for full citations.)

person to grow mental maps of that situation. As Jonathan Haidt[72] points out, based on the work of Gary Marcus:

> The brain is like a book, the first draft of which is written by the genes during fetal development. No chapters are complete at birth, and some are just rough outlines waiting to be filled in during childhood. But not a single chapter—be it on sexuality, language, food preferences, or morality—consists of blank pages upon which a society can inscribe any conceivable set of words.

The conceptual outlines that we rely on to understand the world are created by the pages we are given at birth combined with universal experiences of how human bodies naturally interact with our earthly home.[73] Those outlines serve as robust conceptual foundations that an educated person skillfully applies according to the dictates of their situation through creating mental models that appropriately shape their perceptions, thoughts, actions, and goals. The primary needs are the alphabet that spells out how the outlines are filled in through a combination of cultural patterns and personal choices.

Learning turns out to be complicated by the fact that it can be shallow or deep. Shallow learning is what our school system most consistently produces. Shallow learning is a human default. Our minds tend to maintain existing mental models of ourselves and our situations even in the face of information that contradicts them. In the example of my high school math classes, I was successful at gaming Mr. Schuster's classes because I had mastered the implicit "rules" of classroom schooling. Despite producing "mathematical" behaviors that matched the norms and conventions of Mr. Schuster's homework assignments and tests, my long term mathematical understandings, my mental maps of math concepts, went unchallenged and did not change significantly.

---

[72] Haidt, 2012

[73] Gardner, 2004; Lakoff & Johnson, 1999

New information that contradicts a current mental map is either ignored or dismissed unless we have experienced a strong pattern that suggests that those mental models are failing to help us. Since I was relying on my mental maps of the implicit "rules" of class, not on the implicit "rules" of mathematics, I was consistently successful during my time with Mr. Schuster. My desire was to pass the class; it was not to learn mathematics (though I would not have admitted that at the time because of the norms in that college preparation program). In my junior year I failed, but then was given a way to avoid facing that failure by studying the norms and conventions of the SAT testing process. A pattern of failing to get what we want is the impetus for investing more energy in the learning process. Since I was given the means to avoid confronting my math failures, my mathematical learning was shallow and it remained a subject that I struggled with for many more years.

In order for increased energy investments in learning to reliably pay off, we need to have access to certain psychological states during the learning process. Deeper learning requires us to be in a state of cognitively flexible openness. There may be other factors that can prevent deeper learning, but without openness learning cannot be deep. This openness is most reliably produced when our psychological needs have been satisfied, allowing us to be fully engaged with the activities available within the situation we want to master.

The flow state described by Mihalyi Csikszentmihalyi (me-high chick-sent-me-high) is an example of this openness.[74] The symptoms of the flow state include losing track of time, a sense of oneness that involves losing a sense that you are a separate individual distinct from your activities, and responding to the feedback from the activity without having to consciously think about what to do or how to do it. This state tends to come about when the level of challenge you face from the activity is matched to the level of skill that you bring to it. Too much challenge and you are overwhelmed, too little and you are bored. When you are close to boredom you may be productively engaged, but your learning is shallow. When you are skirting the edge of being

---

[74] Csikszentmihalyi, 2001

overwhelmed, with occasional autonomous forays beyond your abilities, then you are probably learning as effectively and efficiently as possible. Psychological need satisfaction ensures that nothing immediately important to well-being intrudes on your relationship to the activity at hand. Thus the ideal outcome that occurs with this combination is deeper learning.

The situations described in the eight scenarios presented in Chapter 1 would be absurd for all human beings without exception because they each describe the thwarting of a primary human need. Dead, dying, and dozing students don't learn.[75] Anxious and depressed students don't learn deeply, and shallow learning is not enough to prepare children for succeeding in today's complex globalized society. There are other outcomes that are valuable, but if we can't reliably produce deeper learning, then we are babysitting, not educating.

What thwarting of primary human needs undermines is motivation for and engagement with available activities. Motivation refers to the energy that is made available for activities, while engagement is the translation of a person's motivation (energy) into actions that affect their situation. Engagement has four aspects:[76]

- behavioral
- emotional
- cognitive
- agentic

Behavioral engagement refers to deployment of attention, effort, and persistence. *Emotional* engagement is indicated by the presence of positive emotions and the absence of negative emotions during an activity. *Cognitive* engagement means that the learner uses more sophisticated strategies for learning. *Agentic* engagement involves the injection of the

---

[75] Sleep is a crucial component of learning in a broad sense due to the way that it enables the mind to process information for long term storage and perhaps other functions. That said there is no credible evidence that I am aware of to support the idea that external inputs from an instructor could be effectively incorporated into the learning process of a sleeping student.

[76] Reeve, 2013

learner's curiosities, preferences, and opinions into the social processes of interacting with others involved in the activity in order to improve those processes and, ultimately, the educational outcomes.

Output

The crucial output of schooling is supposed to be educated citizens. But what is it about educated citizens that make them more valuable to society? Recall that an educated person is, literally, someone who perceives accurately, thinks clearly, and acts effectively on self-selected goals and aspirations that are appropriate to their situation, without explicitly knowing that those various things are going on. The clue to answering the question is in the phrase "appropriate to their situation." This is where the rubber meets the road in terms of being educated. If you don't understand your situation, then you are not going to be able to respond *appropriately* to it. This was not much of an issue in the past when most of us lived in situations that were not all that different from the hunter-gatherer bands of our earliest ancestors. There is no question that, for most people in our society, life no longer bears much resemblance to the lifestyles of our ancient predecessors. Therein lies the problem with a school system that produces mostly shallow learning. The mental maps we tend to come up with intuitively (via shallow learning) are not very helpful these days. Deeper learning is required in order to properly understand our current situation.

Careers, for instance, are obviously important over the long term for most people, but they should be considered a natural *by-product* of being an educated citizen. The ideal citizen is one who is aware of their situation and formulates and effectively pursues appropriate goals given the means they have available. At the system level it is not relevant whether any given individual gets a job, starts an enterprise, or retreats into a hermitage. What matters for the system is having citizens attuned to making good decisions about what to do based on available opportunities.

The K-12 educational institutions we have inherited from our ancestors were based on the intuitively obvious (but mistaken) notion of educating an atomic self within a knowable universe. You will recall that I am using the phrase "atomic self" to distinguish the useless concept of the "self" as a distinct unit from the more recent concept of the "self" as a useful narrative fiction like the center of gravity of a hoop. The school system is designed to deliver units of "known" academic content about that universe to students who are each assumed to be an atomic self that can take in those units and thereby master that universe. The assumption

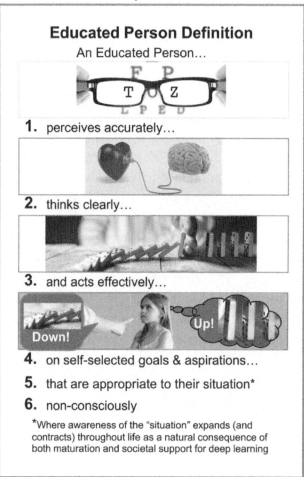

Educated Person Definition
An Educated Person...

1. perceives accurately...

2. thinks clearly...

3. and acts effectively...

4. on self-selected goals & aspirations...

5. that are appropriate to their situation*

6. non-consciously

*Where awareness of the "situation" expands (and contracts) throughout life as a natural consequence of both maturation and societal support for deep learning

is that the atomic self of the student must navigate the requirements of the system; their individual performance is what the system is designed to account for. That atomic self must learn some set of knowledge, skills, and information in the schooling situation and is encouraged to apply it to all other non-school situations. This is the notoriously difficult "transfer problem" that is a consistent thorn in the sides of educators and education researchers.

Likewise, the atomic self of each teacher is charged with becoming increasingly proficient at using a variety of instruction pumps to deliver standardized units of content into their students. This delivery model is illustrated in simplified comic form on the next page. The top section portrays the basic delivery model of education while the lower section shows how it informs the operations of large-scale institutions.

Standardized tests and other forms of instructional bookkeeping are generally regarded as the primary outcomes used to hold everyone "accountable" within this complicated system of content delivery. All that is required to "demonstrate" or "account for" the presence or absence of academic content is the replication of the content (or a "reasonable" semblance of it) in some testing situation. The instructional bookkeeping of grades usually relies on teachers to be accurate assessors of student capabilities. Given the high rates of remediation required of entering college freshmen, their accuracy currently appears to be poor.[77] Given how the makers of the films *A Private Universe* and *Minds of Our Own*[78] recorded graduates and faculty of MIT and Harvard failing simple tests of basic knowledge and Howard Gardner's point that a majority of advanced degree holders at elite institutions fail basic tests,[79] the reliability of the mainstream system for documenting learning should be in question.

The content delivery concept of education is also inherently based on predefining what goals are to be pursued, independent of the situations in which students exist. The process of students generating their own

---

[77] Chen, 2016

[78] HSCA, 1987, 1997

[79] Gardner, 2004 pp. 143-184

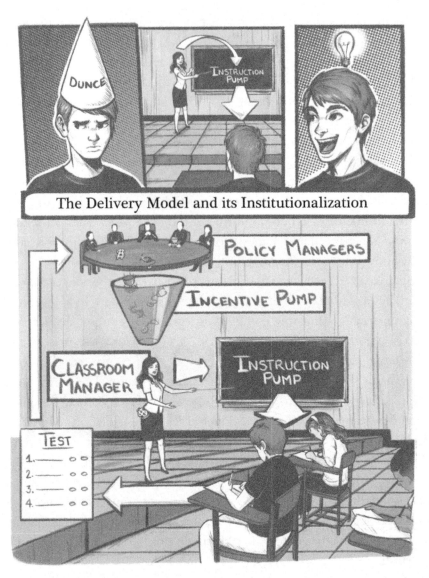

goals and aspirations is largely neglected. Goals are imposed with the effect of preempting productive exploration of the issue of how students' goals and aspirations develop and what educators may be able to do to help students to improve those processes.

The view that learning can be understood as the acquisition and transfer of knowledge is equivalent to Aristotle's "essential elements" view of the physical world which was invalidated by the material sciences.

From a scientific perspective it is no longer sensible to consider the universe knowable (except from the perspective of specific purposes). From the perspective of psychology the idea of an atomic self into or from which content can be delivered is not useful. The mental model of education as content delivery based on atomic selves in a knowable universe does not distinguish between shallow and deep learning and it cannot account for fauxchievement (jumping through the hoops and getting the rewards but staying ignorant). It is also silent with regard to the crucial roles of motivation and engagement in learning and in other human affairs. As a psychologist and educator, I deem these flaws to be fatal.

Education Consistent with Human Nature

In order to clarify a psychological view of human nature and how it is relevant to education, let's recall the basic literal definition presented earlier in the chapter: an educated person is someone who perceives accurately, thinks clearly, and acts effectively on self-selected goals and aspirations that are appropriate to their situation without explicitly knowing that those various things are going on. Over the long term, learning must necessarily improve their processes of setting, pursuing, and adjusting goals and aspirations, as well as improving perception, thought, action, and situational understanding.

To that foundation we can add that humans, along with all the rest of life, are biological systems that are inherently complex and adaptive. The human learning that we collectively pursue in the K-12 arena necessarily entails interactions among a wide variety of biological, psychological, relational, cultural, and social structures, processes, and patterns to become what we individually experience as perception, thought, action, etc. I concur with the Self-Determination Theory (SDT) research community founded by Edward Deci and Richard Ryan that we humans non-consciously pursue an agenda of learning relentlessly as long as we have the capacity to do so.[80] If someone does not appear to be relentless about it, then that person has been trained by the particular context in

---

[80] Deci & Ryan, 1985, 2000; Ryan & Deci, 2000a, 2000b

which they are embedded to consistently expect failure. The most extreme version of being trained out of relentlessly pursuing learning is what psychologists call learned helplessness.[81] As long as a person perceives the situation to be one in which success will be consistently thwarted, then they are most likely to conserve their energy until they perceive an opportunity to succeed. The conservation of energy can be entirely managed through non-conscious processes; thus the individual may not have any conscious notion that they have had their expectations shaped externally nor that their "choices" are being constrained by an internal energy-conserving strategy. In such a situation they will, however, exhibit symptoms of psychological distress such as anxiety, depression, etc.

Humans are always learning, but shallow learning is our default. Shallow learning merely confirms our cognitive models of the world and how it works by generally dismissing or ignoring everything to the contrary. The persistent difficulties we have with our cognitive biases and our numerous systematic thinking errors show that we were never psychologically blank slates.[82]

We have a variety of mental models that are some combination of built-in and learned, with heavy emphasis on learned. When we encounter new situations, we must initially rely on our existing models before we can develop different understandings that may better serve our goals and aspirations. All new models grow out of older models. These are "new" in the sense that the organization is novel, not the component parts that were just re-assembled. Remember the alphabet analogy; even though this book is new there is not a single new letter or word in it. In the same way, new understandings arise out of the rearrangement of bits of experience, not the creation of wholly new bits.

Certain types of changes to our cognitive maps can be energetically expensive when they alter more fundamental features of our perception. For instance, our intuitive notions of the physics of moving ourselves through space and interacting with objects in the world are some of the

---

[81] Seligman, 2002

[82] Ariely, 2008; Kahneman 2011; Pinker, 2002

The Backwards Brain Bicycle
Smarter Every Day 133

Destin Sandlin

most fundamental that we have. When experimental psychologists make subjects wear eyeglasses that alter the orientation of their visual fields like switching left for right or up for down, the subjects eventually adjust but the changes are difficult and the process is disorienting, to the point of nausea and vomiting in at least one case.[83]

Another interesting illustration of how hard it is to alter a deep level of perceptual understanding is The Backwards Brain Bicycle video by Destin Sandlin, host of the Smarter Every Day YouTube channel.[84] After being presented with an apparently impossible-to-ride bicycle that had the steering mechanism reversed, Destin decided to practice until he mastered the task. It took him eight months! Then on a visit to Amsterdam he tried to ride a regular bike and initially failed. The re-re-learning to ride the regular bike only took about twenty minutes. (He also got his five- or six-year-old son to ride a backwards bike too, but you will have to watch the video to find out how long it took!)

[83] Degenaar, 2013; for historical review Sachse, Beermann, Martini, et al., 2017

[84] The Backwards Brain Bicycle - Smarter Every Day 133:
https://www.youtube.com/watch?v=MFzDaBzBlL0

Our perceptual relationship to the world is a deep level of cognitive mapping. We refer to learning as "deep" when it changes our most centrally rooted models of reality. The experiments altering a subject's visual orientation or the ability to ride a bike with backwards steering are tapping into a form of learning that is deeper than normal; everything we take to be real is also potentially subject to modification, although it's not usually as easy as putting on a pair of glasses or having a custom bike made. In order for a deep learning process to be more reliably connected to reality, certain psychological conditions are required, which I will discuss shortly.

Of particular concern to many contemporary educators and education leaders in the mainstream is getting students up to speed in science, technology, engineering, arts, and mathematics disciplines (STEAM) in order to maintain our complex globalized way of life. The mainstream also tends to take as a central concern the development of literacy, numeracy, and a few other "basic skills" as prerequisites to good citizenship and the possibility of pursuing STEAM disciplines. Success, or the lack thereof, in these areas of pursuit are used to frame discussions about improving education without regard for the psychological conditions in which they are pursued. This myopic view of the concerns of education is self-defeating when the psychological conditions produced by those leaders happen to undermine the deeper learning that is necessary for ultimate success.

Mainstream educators tend to take critical thinking, effective action, and disciplinary understanding to be their primary areas of influence on students. Educators do *not* usually concern themselves with the outer edges of that list of features of an educated person: perception and goals and aspirations. Perception is assumed (incorrectly) to be an unchangeable given. Some small amount of attention is given to goals and aspirations, but the school system is organized to provide access to a severely limited range of outcomes. Most teachers are probably inclined to go with the flow by encouraging students to "realistically" limit their goals and aspirations to what the system explicitly offers. High school diploma or General Education Diploma (GED)? College or vocation?

Younger children are generally made to pursue goals and aspirations over which they have even less say.

Fauxchievement

Within schools there is a middle ground of learning that occurs when students pursue the rewards offered for parroting the norms and conventions of the instructional situation *without* engaging with the reality that underlies the subject being taught. As mentioned earlier, this is fauxchievement, the process of going through the motions without mastering the material.

Howard Gardner noted that a substantial body of research has shown that 50-80% of advanced degree holders (Bachelors to Doctorate) across many fields practiced fauxcheivement (though he didn't call it that).[85] Fauxcheivement is a major underappreciated problem that pervades our education system. In a recent book, the economist Bryan Caplan[86] makes a detailed and persuasive case for the idea that most of the value assigned to the symbols of schooling, such as diplomas and degrees, is almost entirely based on *merely signaling* to employers that the holders possess certain desirable characteristics rather than any *actual acquisition* of useful skills and knowledge. But the emerging view of human nature within psychology can provide us with productive new avenues for both appreciating the problem of fauxcheivement and fighting against it.

Educating Humans

Taking our epistemic horizons seriously requires us to approach our knowledge of large-scale systems, like K-12 education, with caution. Our default mappings of large-scale systems, like education or the economy, are likely to be based on whatever features of small-scale systems, like our families or schools, happen to have previously caught our attention. It is unlikely that we would notice the features that could be generalized to large-scale systems or that we would also accurately abstract those features in useful ways. For instance, nearly everyone in our society

85 Gardner, 2004 pp. 143-184

86 Caplan, 2018

carries with him/her the substantially inaccurate delivery model of education. Consequently, we would be wise to be wary about the existing assumptions that are embedded in our educational institutions. As the hidden curriculum demonstration at the end of Chapter 4 suggests, we cannot assume that we each have an accurate grasp of the whole situation even if we can produce a logical, grammatically correct, and coherent account of what we think is going on. We need to take our individual accounts of our situation with a grain of salt and seek the kind of social confirmation that mitigates the most pernicious effects of the hidden curriculum. The most reliable system of social confirmation that we have available is science.

From the perspective of managing the system-as-a-whole, we need to be careful and deliberate when assessing what we need to know about the system. I will not attempt to provide a full accounting of all we need to know, but given that learning is at the core of the enterprise, then that is a logical starting point. The underlying reality in education is first and foremost a psychological reality in which deep learning is required but is susceptible to the deleterious effects of fauxchievement. Therefore, the minimal starting point for a K-12 education system today is creating a feedback loop that is sensitive to the psychological patterns that are most relevant to learning and that has the capacity to monitor and modify the rate of fauxchievement. In other words, we need to make sure that schools are organized and operated in a manner that is consistent with human nature and that is sensitive to the fact that education is currently being systematically undermined by fauxchievement.

No one has discerned the full depths of human nature; however we have discerned enough to start making some clear changes to the feedback systems that guide our K-12 education system. There are eight empirically validated properties of human nature. They are the primary human needs for air, water, food, shelter, sleep, relatedness, autonomy, and competence. I take the first five of these to be entirely non-controversial. For decades, strong empirical support for the other three has been steadily building up under the "Basic Psychological Needs" sub-theory within the Self-Determination Theory (SDT) research tradition in psychology. The first four are physiological needs that are of little concern because they are reasonably well-understood (even though they may also be inadequately supported in some schools). The final four needs are more problematic because of how they are persistently and systematically undermined through the organization and operations of mainstream K-12 schools.

Facilitating deeper learning requires creating psychological conditions in which primary needs are satisfied. The Deep Learning Causality Table on the next page contains two simplified chains of causality based on SDT that go from needs through learning to observable outcomes.

Unfortunately, the evidence suggests that the second causal chain rather than the first is business-as-usual in mainstream K-12 schools. For example, Gallup, the international polling organization, and the Carnegie Foundation[87] agree that disengagement is a central problem in schools today. About 53% of students surveyed by Gallup in 2017 said that they were disengaged.[88] But I suspect that 53% may under-represent the actual impact of disengagement because the Gallup poll is taken only once per year and the question is asked in a simple manner that seems unlikely to capture the full extent of the phenomenon for students. For instance, it is entirely unable to detect when a student might be engaged in some classes but disengaged in others. Helen Marks[89] cited several studies in her literature review that found disengagement ranged from 40% to 60% of students (excluding dropouts and repeated absentees). Miller, Latham, & Cahill gathered a set of experts who estimated the rate of student disengagement to be about 60%.[90] My estimation, detailed in the introduction is that 65-75% of students are disengaged. There is a wide variety of other organizations and experts that explicitly endorse deeper learning and so at least implicitly agree that engagement is at issue.[91] A

[87] Headden & McKay, 2015

[88] Gallup, 2017

[89] Marks, 2000

[90] Miller, Latham & Cahill, 2017

[91] AEE, n.d.; Bellanca, 2015; Berry, 2016; Dunleavy & Milton, 2010; Fullan & Quinn, 2016; Kim, 2015; Kysilko, 2014; Mehta & Fine, 2015; Miller, Latham & Cahill, 2016; NPDL, n.d.; Robinson & Aronica, 2016; Zhao, 2009

variety of researchers have observed persistent systematic declines in the engagement and intrinsic motivation of students both within and across the years of K-12 schooling.[92] As mentioned earlier, according to Gallup 70% of teachers are also disengaged.[93]

Deep Learning Causality Table

Ideal

Psychologically Supportive Environment

Needs Satisfied

More Internal Motivations

Full Engagement

Deep Learning

Better Observed Outcomes

Status Quo

Psychologically Negligent Environment

Needs Unsatisfied

More External Motivations

Partial Engagement

Shallow Learning

Worse Observed Outcomes

---

[92] Bouffard, Marcoux, Vezeau, et al., 2003; Corpus, McClintic-Gilbert & Hayenga, 2009; Gottfried, Fleming & Gottfried, 2001; Harter, 1981; Hunter & Csikszentmihalyi, 2003; Lepper, Corpus & Iyengar, 2005; Otis, Grouzet & Pelletier, 2005; Pintrich, 2003; Prawat, Grissom & Parish, 1979; Wigfield, Eccles & Rodriguez, 1998

[93] Hastings & Agrawal, 2015

This particular disconnect is not going to be overcome by merely telling the stories of how clever psychological researchers like Walter Mischel have been tricking people into or out of using their minds in successful ways and then getting educators to use those tricks, too. The disconnect will persist as long as the system is guided by the idea that humans are atomic selves that need to have more units of knowledge (or character traits) delivered into their heads (or hearts) and transferred into the rest of their lives. A proper connection will occur when the K-12 system is guided by the view of human nature that is emerging from psychology. Our school system must learn how to work with the implications of the fact that all human beings are complex adaptive systems that are embodied by and embedded within other complex adaptive systems.

We are inherently programmed to pursue our primary human needs. Those cognitive programs operate outside of our awareness. The programs contribute to the creation of the narrative center of gravity, a self, but the conscious experiencing self does not have any inherently reliable knowledge of its own creation. Those programs, along with our individual experiential history coupled to cultural and social influences, inform how we construct our understanding of what opportunities and limitations exist in the situations in which we find ourselves.[94] Based on our understanding of how we identify ourselves in relation to our situation, we develop a set of preferences. For example, an American male age 51 who works as an urban elementary school principal can be expected to have very different preferences than a Chinese female age 15 who works in her family's rural vegetable stand. Our preferences inform the choices we make about how to engage with the situation, with the level of energy varying according to how our motivation is distributed across a spectrum from other- to self-determined. If the principal had aspirations to a very different kind of life, then the energy he invests in his principalship might be very low and his subsequent learning quite shallow despite the objectively observable privileges and relative wealth he enjoys. The teenage vegetable seller, on the other hand, might put

---

[94] Sapolsky, 2018

tremendous energy into her activities and attain deeper learning because she aspires to taking over and growing the family business someday. The more self-determined our activities, the more energy we invest in those activities and the deeper our learning can be.

All of our perceptions, thoughts, actions, understandings, and goals and aspirations are inexorably shaped one way or another by our primary needs in entirely non-conscious ways. Primary needs are default non-conscious meta-goals. Independent of the situation in which we find ourselves, we all pursue the means to express our autonomy, competence, and relatedness. Each culture provides various ways in which those means can be pursued and how much those various means are valued, but all humans are concerned about finding ways to express themselves through meeting their primary needs.

Our complex adaptive creativity (adaptivity) is oriented to satisfying primary needs, but neither our adaptivity nor our needs are directly accessible to the conscious "self" which is experiencing our lives. In America and other Western countries our cultures value individuality and our narratives about freedom enshrine it for some as a sacred value. In East Asian cultures, belonging is valued such that it may also reach the level of sacredness.[95] Some of the tensions between American and Chinese cultures may arise because of the apparent difference in those values. However, the psychological evidence suggests that, ideological assertions aside, Chinese people need autonomy[96] and Americans need to belong.[97] Our narratives about how we experience the world are going to indirectly reflect the concerns of primary need satisfaction, but with the vast variety of biological, psychological, relational, cultural, and societal influences that affect those narratives, we cannot assume that they will do so in easily predictable ways.

The concern for creating the conditions necessary for deeper learning requires us to take the experiences of learners seriously. From the large-

---

[95] Nisbett, 2007

[96] Bao & Lam, 2008

[97] Chen, Vansteenkiste, Beyers, Boone, Deci, et.al, 2015; Deci, Ryan, Gagné, Leona, Usunov, & Kornazheva, 2001

scale systems management perspective, we need to optimize engagement. There are four types of measures that are well established within SDT research which will be useful for assessing the soundness of the foundations for deeper learning within schools:

1. **Need Support:** Objective observations of how need support is provided by others
2. **Need Satisfaction:** How well each individual reports having their needs satisfied by those circumstances
3. **Motivation:** The pattern of motivations reported by individuals for the activities in which they participate (along a spectrum from self- to other-determined)
4. **Engagement:** The pattern of engagement observed and/or reported with the learning opportunities individuals encounter (across four aspects: behavioral, emotional, cognitive, and agentic)

Our assessments of primary need satisfaction, motivation, and engagement need to be carefully informed by scientific practices that take into account our human propensity to creatively distort our memories and the self-serving ways we tend to explain the experiences of others.[98] There are challenges associated with gathering each kind of data, so there is not a single dataset that will provide us with exactly the information we need. However, strategic use of these types of data can enable us to cost effectively improve the psychological conditions within our school system. These are the data we need to have flowing through the system as feedback about how well the psychological conditions within schools align with the deeper learning that is needed. These are the "fuel gauges" for deeper learning.

---

[98] Ariely, 2008; Gilbert, 2006; Kahneman, 2011

Deeper Learning Theory

The following steps are at the core of the process of deeper learning: activate a cognitive map for the purpose being pursued, engage enthusiastically enough to expose flaws in the map, and then revise the map to better reflect the world of that pursuit. Three comics coming up will illustrate how starting with the same basic external observation of a student ignorant of how to effectively pursue a purpose they have chosen can lead to the three different broad outcomes observed in our school system. The learning process is depicted as having three stages which can produce different outcomes depending on how the learning process goes.

The first variation shown on the next page is the deep learning ideal in which the process is connected to the reality of a subject matter. The ignorant student is presented with a situation that activates his mental map of the phenomena in question (illustrated as a treasure in the student's mind and the activation of a puzzle map depicting the goal). Next the student engages with the topic (illustrated as the assembly of a treasure map from the puzzle pieces). When the student is unable to achieve his goal (illustrated as a failure caused by puzzle pieces that are missing and improperly oriented) then he will have an opportunity to re-map his understanding. The quality of the new map will vary according to a combination of the quality of the feedback and the quality of the engagement with that feedback (illustrated as the incompleteness of the final map that enabled partial success). The final outcome is a student enlightened with regard to that particular aspect of the subject matter (illustrated by the student wearing the crown in his mind). Notice that the instructional process (illustrated by the inset panels showing an adult) is optional, meaning that it may or may not be included in the sequence of events observed and, even if it did occur, it may or may not play a role in the actual learning. Good instruction, in which primary needs are supported, is a likely source of both map activations and high quality feedback for the re-mapping process, so designating the instructional process as optional does not diminish the value of instruction.

Deeper Learning

The second variation in this sequence is labelled Fauxchievement. The key difference is in the activation of a goal to attain some form of reward or benefit rather than actually understanding the topic at hand

Fauxchievement

(illustrated as the gift of a grade in the foreground separated from the subject matter treasure in the background). This occurs when a student perceives the instructional bookkeeping that is valued by the system as more valuable than understanding the subject matter or else there is a failure to maintain the connection of the subject matter to reality. When the system fails in this way the feedback a student receives is arbitrarily generated by the norms and conventions of the schooling process, not the underlying reality of the subject matter. Students are engaged, but in the wrong way. They expend energy and effort, but it is wasted because the students are merely "playing the game" or "jumping through the hoops" instead of fully engaging with the reality behind the subject matter, like I did in my high school math classes. In the end I was happy to have the system-approved "evidence" of my "learning," but I was functionally still ignorant about the reality of what was "taught." In other words, my naïve unworkable concepts about the reality of math remained largely unchanged as the system falsely declared me to be educated in those matters. The girl in the comic is satisfied with her grade but the truth is that the gift of a mere grade is devoid of real value (depicted as the empty gift box in the final panel).

The third variation shown on the next page is labelled Shallow Learning. In this scenario the student discovers that her goals and aspirations are simply irrelevant to what goes on in the school setting (portrayed as a mismatch between the student's goal of "O", the puzzle map that was activated with the goal "X," and the world). Through various means of compulsion that may be more or less gentle, she is forced to do things that she has little or no interest in doing (portrayed in the fourth panel as envisioning herself as imprisoned). One or more of her primary human psychological needs are being thwarted. As a result, she has poor motivation and over time is likely to become more and more disengaged. If the compulsions are sufficiently gentle she may not even realize that her motivation is deficient. If the compulsions are too ham-handed then she is likely to be negatively labelled and/or to become alienated, with dropping out subsequently becoming an increasingly likely possibility. The intellectual result is the preservation of unworkable ideas about the world (portrayed as the student in the fifth

Shallow Learning

panel having an inaccurate map and being angry and hopeless in the final panel; envisioning herself as a dead person imprisoned forevermore).

Marshmallow Test Revisited

Let's return to the Marshmallow Test to explore the changes in our understanding that arise from this new perspective on human nature informed by epistemic horizons, primary needs, and deeper learning. First we have to come up with a different kind of description for the experimental situation. The experiments were originally framed, and are still popularly described, as being about willpower and/or impulsivity. This is misleading. The experiments actually demonstrated the development and consequences of certain cognitive abilities in children. Children who are that young have limited executive control. The suite of cognitive functions that fall under the phrase "executive control" are more numerous than those covered by this particular experimental paradigm, but there has not been sufficient research to be more precise.[99] The children are embodied by biological structures that are inherently capable of developing further in these regards and are embedded in a situation that is explicitly designed to place a significant burden on those particular biological structures. The experiment presents children with a variety of situational constraints that may or may not tax that subset of executive functions. Popular accounts of this experimental paradigm tend to ignore what was revealed about a child's exquisite sensitivity to the situation when making a decision. A careful reading of the experiments reveals situational manipulations that help or hinder the decisions of the children. The long term predictive or diagnostic power of specific situations suggests how *helpful or unhelpful* some of the situational manipulations were. For example, when the experimenters made suggestions of how to think about the marshmallows as "puffy clouds," that input enabled otherwise "impulsive" children to transform their performance from an average of about five minutes into an average of thirteen minutes.[100] In education parlance, the experimenters found several ways to provide scaffolding that enhanced the children's performance, but only temporarily. The scaffolding improved the performance in the moment, but had no noticeable long term effect.

---

[99] Peake, 2017 p. 52

[100] Ayduk, 2007 p. 101

It is important to note that the children were challenged to make an *appropriate* choice about whether to consume the immediately available smaller and less preferred option or to wait for the larger and more preferred option. It is important to recognize that the option of waiting longer is *not* always the most optimal choice. It is highly adaptive (that is, rational) to choose the shorter waiting time when there is a reasonable chance that the larger and more preferred option is not reliably going to be delivered. It would be irrational and counterproductive to invest in that wait when there is a fair chance that the preferred option will not be delivered as promised. Given the basic meaning of being an educated person presented earlier, then *the core of K-12 schooling is the development of rational adaptivity.* We need to be able to meaningfully adapt ourselves to the realities in which we are embedded. K-12 schooling needs to be a system for attuning children to using all their senses, emotions, thoughts, and behavior to better understand and productively react to reality. Do not be misled by my use of the term "rational" here; I am advocating the use of all our human sensibilities to confront reality. The only way that we can achieve the right balance among those various sensibilities will be through deeper learning.

This is a new way of conceiving of the schooling situation. A child's use of executive functions to better assess and appropriately respond to any given situation in which they find themselves is the central concern. For example, instead of being primarily concerned about the development of "basic skills" in the early grades, we should instead be primarily concerned about creating a sufficiently enriched environment for the children to pursue self-selected goals and aspirations without having to worry about any of their primary needs. Children's executive functions must have content in order to work, so this is about having appropriate content available for them *and* simultaneously stimulating the development of their cognitive processing capabilities as they make choices about that content.

Academic skills should be considered a set of culturally significant tools that are available to be used as part of a repertoire of adaptation. Academic tools and skills for using them have no value for a learner in the absence of a purpose that they can serve. Only after academic tools are seen *by a child* as the most appropriate ones for accomplishing *their* purposes does the child's construction and use of those tools become a legitimate issue for educators. Prior to the child's realization of the value of academics, the only legitimate educational issue is how they are developing and pursuing their goals and aspirations. Rather than being concerned about academic transfer, we should concern ourselves with situational awareness and cognitive flexibility in the form of appropriate goals and aspirations that are being pursued effectively. It is likely that executive functions more readily transcend situations than content does; therefore making the stimulation of executive functions a higher priority may be the key to solving many educational problems, like the notoriously difficult academic transfer problem.

I am a fan of the "radical" schools that identify themselves as democratic because my sense is that their overarching commitment to providing clear navigable social structures may hold the key to executive function stimulation systems. The democratic schools that have survived for more than a decade seem to share the practice of putting conflict resolution systems and collective decision-making systems (which can both produce and resolve conflicts) at the center of how they operate. Which is not to say that I think putting those systems in the *center* is necessary. What is needed are robust social systems that can, when necessary, take the center of attention by overriding academic processes. The most teacher-centric pedagogical practices advocated by educational conservatives, like E.D. Hirsch,[101] could be the most effective, but we will only find out after we have established a proper base-line of comparison across groups of students that share similar levels of primary human need support, motivation, and engagement. In other words, we will only be able to truly compare the effectiveness of teaching practices by studying groups of students who are embedded in social systems that honor their human nature by consistently stimulating their executive functions. The radically progressive democratic schools, without saying so, seem to provide that support as their primary pedagogical

---

[101] The education conservative who famously wrote a series of books that claims to spell out exactly what every American child "needs to know" at each grade level from preschool to sixth grade.

commitment. It remains to be seen from a scientific perspective whether some version of educationally conservative schooling can strike the right balance of social and academic structure. (To be fair, there is not enough data on the kinds of progressive schools I favor to be 100% certain of my claims. I am, as a psychologist, confident that I make errors, but in this case my errors are probably trivial.)

Our updated view of human nature means that we may be able to reframe some of the experimental manipulations of the Marshmallow Test as varied levels of support for autonomy, relatedness, and competence. The outcomes of these experimental situations are considered diagnostic of long term cognitive functioning in the children when primary needs seem to be supported. This suspicion that primary need manipulations could largely account for the effects of the old experimental manipulations should be empirically confirmed. Another next step for research is to test the hypothesis that executive function stimulation through implementing particular social systems for decision making, conflict resolution, and deeper learning may be the keys to altering those long term outcomes.[102]

One intervention to consider is making instruction available *only* upon request, not imposed as a situational constraint as is typical in mainstream schooling. This is a practice that is implemented in hundreds of schools around the world that typically self-identify as democratic schools; the most well-known examples being A.S. Neill's Summerhill School in

---

[102] Experimentally testing this hypothesis would involve immersing children in situations in which their primary needs are consistently supported and their executive functions are challenged (or not) on a regular basis over time. It is possible that executive function is not susceptible to long term changes until later in child development; therefore, it would be informative to have the manipulation occur for different groups of children in different periods of childhood and adolescence. This experimental paradigm requires first that a system of pervasive psychological need support is created and maintained. Second, a system of executive function stimulation through social systems for decision-making, conflict resolution, and deeper learning needs to be developed that is consistent with that need support system. The experimental manipulations should include methods of self-determined development of goals and aspirations, in particular. The expectation is that children with more executive function stimulation in the context of pervasive need support would get better at pursuing and attaining their self-selected goals and aspirations.

Leiston, Suffolk, England, and Sudbury Valley School in Framingham, MA, USA.

Given the fact that instructors are also humans conceived of in the same way as children, they will be optimally functional (or learn to be) to the degree that they are 1) equally entitled to having their preferences honored in 2) the context of pervasive primary need support within 3) a situation that expects them to live within the epistemic horizon bubble that they are actively constructing on a day-to-day basis. Naturally, in order to be optimally effective, regardless of an instructor's pedagogical training, the instructor needs to adapt to the situation in which they find themselves. In this case they need to figure out how to align their pedagogical choices to the children they actually encounter. No matter what pedagogical choice is made, if it is unresponsive to the children who are supposed to learn from it, then it will not be optimally effective. This may require some negotiation between instructors and students if the pedagogical preferences of the instructors don't happen to be an ideal match to the preferences and lifestyles of those students.[103] The distinction between this context for learning and the current mainstream context of classroom schooling is the high value placed on the responsiveness between the adults and children in the instructional situation. This responsiveness is what naturally follows from the idea that humans are inherently complex relational beings, not atomic units that are making and taking deliveries.

Taking a psychological perspective on learning informs my belief in the second element of the Back to Basics 2.0 set of strategies: manage for engagement, not obedience. Understand that obedience will happen, but it is not helpful to use it as a gauge of effective educational management. Obedience is less important than having students and teachers attuned to the well-being of themselves and their fellow community members, how their situations are affecting all that well-being, and how they can use their power to make the situation more supportive of everyone's well-being.

---

[103] Emdin, 2017; Toshalis, 2016

In the final chapter I propose a method for creating the kind of organizational opening that is necessary for productive change. The method is a policy resolution that needs to be backed up with organizational activism. But before we go there I want to address the context in which that activism is situated.

6 E PLURIBUS UNUM

Destructive divisiveness is a major global issue and it is as rampant in the field of education as anywhere else. The resurgence of movements promoting hate and separatism are putting humanity at risk of losing many of the battles some may have thought were already effectively won: social stability through political and religious pluralism, the elimination of mass violence, defeating the ravages of disease, and universal literacy. A long established pattern of successful changes for the better on the global scale appear to have brought with it the seeds of its own destruction.

Assuming that we are embedded within and embodied by complex adaptive systems gives support to the adjacent possible path towards the impossible as a model of the real world. This particular systems view also provides the aspiration to unity amidst diversity (e puribus unum) new urgency. The rise of divisiveness globally and the incoherence of classroom practice can be thought of as a symptoms of transitional states that will eventually give way to new forms of coherence and stability. I am banking on the possibility that the solid empirically supported facts about primary human needs can provide the basis for coherence and stability that is better for all humans, rather than some other alternative that might make many humans' experiences worse. I assume that the complex adaptive creativity (adaptivity) that has created today's global challenges is also inherently capable of becoming aligned across multiple levels of the system to solve them. Recognizing how seemingly contradictory views can be and have previously been reconciled is one way to approach catalyzing that kind of change.

Educational Relativity

Partisanship can take a variety of forms. In politics there are the long-standing parties that define the sides. In education there are partisans that have nothing to do with political party affiliations.[104] To help you understand what this kind of partisanship involves let me tell you a story.

The education world is in the situation of having to solve two relativity problems. A "relativity problem" is one in which there are a variety of different views of the situation and they each seem to be mutually incompatible with the others, even though they are each making true and accurate observations of the same underlying reality.

Recall the imagined debate about squareness among ancient geometers from Chapter 4. As I said, the original terms of the debate must be transcended. The solution is to formulate a unified conception that establishes the interrelationship between the previously opposed sides.

In case you are skeptical of the plausibility of the geometer story consider some other debates about hidden realities in which a set of logically contradictory stories turned out to be correct and it was the logic of contradiction itself which was in error. Consider the debate in physics over whether light is a wave or a particle. The debate itself goes back to the ancient Greeks. Finally, the double slit experiment that settled the debate was created in the nineteenth century. The experiment is based on the idea that if you randomly shoot discreet objects (say marbles) towards a wall through a screen with two parallel slits in it, after a while the marbles hitting the wall will accumulate into a pattern that vaguely

---

[104] As E.D. Hirsch explained, "I am a political liberal, but once I recognized the relative inertness and stability of the shared background knowledge students need to master reading and writing, I was forced to become an educational conservative.... Logic compelled the conclusion that achieving the democratic goal of high universal literacy would require schools to practice a large measure of educational traditionalism." (Moore, 2010)

The Double Slit Experiment

Discrete objects make just
two lines similar to the slits.

Waves make many lines of
diminishing strength from the center.

resembles two parallel lines similar to the slits in your screen. However, if you were to send continuous waves through the screen then the pattern on the wall would be a long series of lines across the wall called an interference pattern. An interference pattern occurs because the peaks and troughs of the waves are radiating outwards from the slits in curves that are centered at each slit. Where the peak of a wave from one slit meets the peak of a wave from the other slit then the result is a higher peak. The same happens to the troughs, when they meet they reinforce each other. Where a peak meets a trough, then they cancel each other out. Since waves move in curves, parallel lines still appear on the wall but there are many of them in diminishing strength from the center. When this experiment was first done the pattern on the wall was an interference pattern, suggesting that light must be a wave.

At that time the particle theory was associated with bigwig scientists like Sir Isaac Newton and there were many more proponents on his side. They found it absurd that one of the mathematical implications of the wave theory was that a single photon could be passing through both slits simultaneously. In order to address this possibility directly they set up an experiment in which they would not just observe the pattern on the wall, but the slit, too. They would determine which slit the photon passed through. When they did that experiment they saw which slit the photon went through, but when they looked at the wall it did not show the spread of lines indicating interference; it was a pair of lines. The additional observation changed the result of the experiment, which blew their minds. It turned out that light is both a wave and a particle, depending on how it is observed. The famous physicist Werner Heisenberg wrote, "[T]he measuring device has been constructed by the observer, and we have to remember that what we observe is not nature in itself but nature exposed to our method of questioning."

Another debate along these lines is about whether our behavior is caused by our genes (nature) or by how we learn from our experiences of the world (nurture). The nature versus nurture debate was given that name by Francis Galton, Charles Darwin's cousin. The discovery of epigenetics settled this debate. What epigenetics revealed is that genes can be turned on or off by experiences with the world. Genes switching on and off is expected; what was completely unexpected was that you can have one of your genes switched and then that new *position* for the gene switch can be passed down to your children and grandchildren. Again what was once a logically either/or question was resolved because reality insisted on both/and. Our behavior is determined by both our genes and our learning, it is both nature and nurture.

The problem of practice in education is often framed as if it must be centered on either the student or the teacher. There is also a less well-recognized problem occurring at the level of values.

Policy prescriptions for improvement to K-12 education are famous for swinging back and forth between encouraging practice to be student- or teacher-centered. This is the K-12 political pendulum problem.

Larry Cuban's history of classroom practice, *How Teachers Taught: Constancy and Change in American Schools 1890-1990, Second Edition*, was a scholarly attempt to figure out where system-wide teaching practice started out in 1890 and where it ended up a hundred years later.[105] In order to ensure that he could capture something useful amongst a diverse set of observational data, Cuban focused on the prevalence of specific practices that were generally recognized as central features of either teacher- or student-centric pedagogy. The century started off with the complete dominance of teacher-centered practice in public schools, then

---

[105] Cuban, 1993 (See References for full citations.)

despite widespread enthusiasm for the adoption of student-centered pedagogy at various times during that period, there were still very few examples of it by 1990. The largest scale of adoption was at the elementary school level, where it was present in a minority of schools and rarely in pure form. His analysis suggests that there were easily identifiable tidal forces at work in the system that continually reset the behavioral beachhead of the classroom to that teacher-centric starting point.

Putting Cuban's historical perspective on teaching practice into the jargon of educational change, there was only marginal adoption of student-centered pedagogy and fidelity to the original design intentions was low. This means that the innovators have had very little substantive effect. Schools are still largely teacher-centric despite multiple waves of so-called progressive innovation to get them to be more student-centric.

Educational conservatives who champion the teacher-centered traditions see the ways that the system falls short and blames it on how we've deviated from what they consider to be rigorous instructional practices. They seem to figure that the techniques that appear to have been effective in the past have become less effective because of how things have changed after the waves of progressivism. Their attitude seems to be that if students would just suck it up and do what skillful instructors tell them to do, then the school system would be better.

On the other hand, the advocates of student-centered teaching practices tend to recognize how boring and repulsive it is for children to be made to do academic activities when there are so many other fun ways that kids could be learning. They still want the kids to learn the academics, but they want the teachers and the system writ-large to be more accommodating to what children are naturally like as immature human beings and how their cultural and personal circumstances may alter how receptive they are to academic traditions.

Some version of these sentiments have been pushing and pulling the policies of schools for well over a hundred years and, no matter what has been done, the results have consistently been only marginal improvements. While the progressives that have been focused on getting classrooms to be more student-centered have made *some* inroads into a

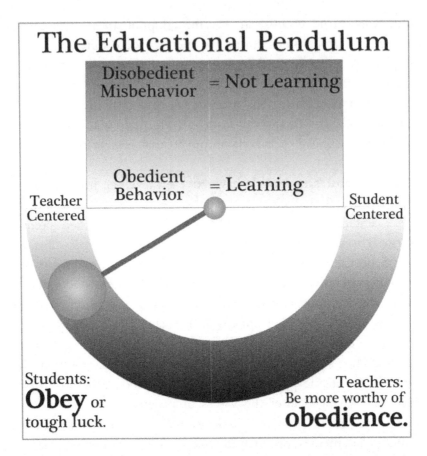

The Educational Pendulum

Disobedient Misbehavior = Not Learning

Obedient Behavior = Learning

Teacher Centered

Student Centered

Students: **Obey** or tough luck.

Teachers: Be more worthy of **obedience.**

system that was almost entirely teacher-centric in the 1890's, Cuban observes that teacher-centric practices still dominate, even if some people in the schools may say they don't.

First off, there are a few things that everyone seems to agree on. Everyone who has been setting education policy since forever agrees that 1) basic academics are the first priority, 2) in order to be educated the kids must be instructed, and 3) in the context of that instruction, they are either learning or they are not. From this point of view we can tell if they are learning by whether or not they obey the teacher. Obedient compliance with the instructions of the adults in a classroom leads to learning. Obedience can mean sucking it up and doing what you are told regardless of your feelings. Or, obedience can mean obeying instructors who have taken the time to get to know you and to develop your trust in them so you believe they truly have your best interests at heart. Either way, disobedient misbehaviors are generally regarded as an indication that there is a lack of learning. This is the commonsense one-dimensional notion behind education policy today (illustrated on the previous page).

However, that commonsense notion fails to account for what we actually know about learning from the discoveries in cognitive psychology since the 1970's. Over the past 50 years we have discovered that this notion of learning as indistinguishable from obedience can undermine our ability to make good decisions about how to run schools (and society). The rampant disengagement in both schools and society shows this.

One basic fact that psychologists uncovered is that "not learning" only happens when you are dead, severely ill, or asleep. So, we must drop the notion that "not learning" is even worth considering in the school context.

What we need to consider is whether learning is shallow or deep. Humans default to shallow learning, which means we are only open to taking in information that fits with how we already understand things. Under the right circumstances we can learn deeply. The concept of deeper learning was explained in chapter 5; you may recall the Backwards Brain Bicycle an example illustrating one form of conceptual depth.

If we attempt to assimilate information that does not fit with our current understanding in the right way, by opening our mind such that it enables us to reorganize our understanding, then the result is deeper learning. Learning deeply is especially crucial to being a good citizen in our globalized society today.

Once this idea of deeper versus shallow learning is in place, then it is obvious that properly structuring the instructional process is crucial to success. In the 60's and 70's there were some efforts to "eliminate structure" in some experiments that called themselves "free schools." But nearly all of those schools failed and no longer exist. The few that survive still rhetorically reject academic structure, but have figured out how to provide a robust social structure that protects the academic "freedom" for students; this forms the basis of their approach to education.

Attitude 1ˢᵗ Continuum
Predicting the Outcomes of Learning

Quality of Experience

| | Traumatized | Bored | Enthusiastic |

The question of the quality of academic structures was famously quantified by education researcher Benjamin Bloom in what he called the 2-sigma challenge. He and his students found that one-on-one tutoring, an obviously highly student-centric practice, was far more effective than the baseline of the traditional teacher-centric practice of delivering lectures. They found that a set of techniques called "mastery" learning was about half way between the two, which led to a whole host of schools adopting the mastery method. The results were only marginal improvements when examined across diverse implementations with varying fidelity to the original design, par for the course of K-12 innovation.[106]

Part of the problem is that the deeper versus shallow dichotomy is still a single dimension that does not deal with the reality of fake learning

---

[106] Despite Bloom and his colleagues making valiant attempts to find some innovative combination of instructional techniques that could achieve a similarly impressive level of achievement, they failed. I suggest that was the case because they did not appear to make a useful distinction between academic and social structures and therefore never systematically varied the social structures in which the academic structures were offered. (Bloom, 1984)

in which students obediently jump through the hoops without mastering the material. Current mainstream schooling does not yet know how to deal with the fact that some apparently good structures can still fail to produce the proper understanding that we expect.

Drawing on what we can learn from the science of psychology, let's draw out a more realistic picture of how we can understand the outcomes that actually occur in education. We will maintain the notion of structure as a dimension, with good structure on top and poor structure on the bottom of our continuum, shown on the previous page (with the caveat that there are multiple types of structure operating simultaneously.)

Our second dimension is the quality of the experience that the learner is having. Ideally students have enthusiasm. Moving away from the ideal we can see that some students will be in the neutral middle, perhaps bored, but in any case their experience is neither good nor bad. At the other extreme of this dimension is having a bad experience, which is traumatic. It may be either a currently bad experience, or it could be the memory of one. Regardless, learning cannot be deep when the experience is bad.

Let's go through the highlights of what this leads us to expect in terms of outcomes. First, we take the ideal of a good structure that students engage with enthusiastically. The participants would find that their activities are personally challenging and they have access to the state of mind known as flow;[107] described in Chapter 5.

Second, we consider what would happen when there is poor structure with a lack of enthusiasm. That is when the activities are personally unchallenging or just irrelevant. This produces shallow learning.

Next, what does it mean when the learning activity is well-structured but there is still a lack of enthusiasm. Even with good structure the larger context in which the participant is situated may cause some of his or her primary needs to be thwarted instead of supported. This also produces shallow learning.

The final combination is what happens when you have enthusiasm but the structure of your situation is poor. This happens when the

---

[107] Csikszentmihalyi, 2001

feedback from the situation is irrelevant to the goals that participants have. In my own schooling this was a common pattern. Remember how I was able to get decent grades from Mr. Schuster, my sophomore year math teacher. Then, the next year I failed the assessment tests for my junior year so completely that it was as if I had not taken Mr. Schuster's classes at all. I got credit for both classes despite the fact that the ultimate educational purposes of both classes were ultimately defeated. This is an example of fauxcheivement, or fake learning, which means lacking mastery yet still getting credit.

This continuum provides us with a pretty good account of the various types of outcomes that are commonly observed in schools today. The patterns of shallow and fake learning indicate various degrees of disengagement, while the pattern of deeper learning indicates the rare times when engagement prevails. Remember that this is a continuum of outcomes across two dimensions; they are not discrete and they are not necessarily easy to discern one from another.

When we organize schools with this continuum in mind we are going to be putting attitude first instead of academics, but with the full confidence that the academics will follow as long as the students are in touch with the reality that makes academics valuable. The challenge is to make sure that the students are having good experiences, that they have some enthusiasm for what they are doing, as they encounter a reality that they can master through deeper learning.

Recall the political pendulum problem. Why has swinging back and forth between teacher-centric and student-centric classroom instructional practices been such an unreliable means of improving the system? Let's consider how the two different ideological stances portray themselves and their opposition.

Taking the student-centered ideology first, I suggest that they are mostly concerned about the "quality of experience" dimension of the continuum. This would seem to be a good idea. However, they sometimes frame their political opponents in ways that prevent cooperation. If they accuse their opponents of perpetuating evils, like the school-to-prison pipeline and antiquated industrial-age management, they are likely short-changing the legitimate concerns of their opposition.

Proponents of the teacher-centered ideology seem to be concerned with the structure dimension. This also seems like a good idea until they frame their political enemies as perpetuators of classroom chaos and wastefully bloated bureaucracy.

These rhetorical strategies are a manifestation of the broader pattern of divisiveness that is occurring in society. Divisive rhetoric precludes from consideration measures that might appear to be supportive of the "other side." Cooperation is regarded as betrayal. In both cases they do not accurately characterize what the other side is actually trying to achieve, with the result that some useful combinations of ideas that might arise from aligning their agendas for cooperation become politically untenable.

Both sides are basically right about what they *want* to achieve but they do not take into account how the two dimensions work together. When the well-intentioned changes get put into policies without any insight into the actual multi-dimensional complexity of educating children, then they risk only achieving progress in one dimension. With particularly strong rhetoric they might even prevent progress or cause declines in the other dimension. Without a proper insight into multi-dimensionality, they will not set up a system of guidance that can achieve reliable progress toward the true goal of deeper learning. Both sides of the political spectrum are advocating for potentially valuable changes, but they tend not to frame their goals and policies in appropriate ways to take advantage of the reality of learning.

What our education system needs is simultaneous progress in terms of both good structures and good experiences. And that is going to require more than mere obedience from teachers and students. It is going to require them to become more engaged in the process of making productive changes in practice.

The second relativity problem has to do with values, where there are three sides vying for dominance. The dominant authoritarian side argues for Accountability by Standards and Testing, the communitarian side argues for Social Justice and Equity, and the marginalized libertarian side argues for Freedom. Everyone assumes agreement with the following notions: the classroom/school environment should provide access to 1)

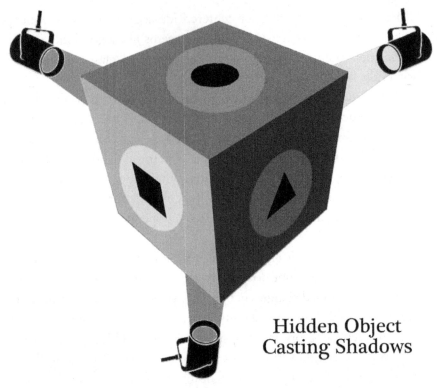

Hidden Object
Casting Shadows

unpolluted air, 2) fresh clean water, 3) healthy food (sent from home by parents, if necessary), 4) shelter from extreme environmental conditions, and 5) enough sleep (though families are usually expected to be the exclusive providers of adequate support for this one at home, which may be a problematic assumption in some cases).

The policies and practices that follow from the dominant authoritarian view have tended to exclude policies and practices that would follow from the other points of view. In the fight to get their views to be legitimized, the non-dominant factions have tended to articulate their positions as incompatible with the dominant position. The dynamics of communicating an ideological position has pushed them to self-define in a manner that emphasizes the distinctions, leading to the implicit suggestion that their perspectives are incompatible with each other.

To give this a more concrete expression consider the picture above. There is an object hidden from view (see p. 126 for the reveal). The object casts three different shadows onto the three sided screen that surrounds it. There are people who are charged with describing the hidden object. In the confusion of a large number of people trying to describe it, the stories that resonate the most tend to dominate in the public sphere. In this case three simple stories were the most compelling because the reality is so complex and difficult to grasp. In a world in which political communication is resistant to complexity and nuance it is much easier to score a victory when your solution can be described in a single word. The policies that follow from saying education is a "pyramid," a "cube," or a "sphere" are more successful than those that offer more complex descriptions. Any new story that comes along and attempts to incorporate more than one view must overcome the resistance to change that is inherently built into long-established "one-word" policies and practices that have evolved over decades to protect themselves from the other ideologies.

As I mentioned before, this has been a recurring theme in the sciences. Both physics and biology have had to accept both/and propositions when both sides of apparently contradictory issues found support for their favored aspect but failed to convincingly negate the position of their rivals. Light is both a wave and a particle. Our behavior is caused by both our genetic inheritance and what we learn from our environment.

I propose that in education we need to consider that there are true and correct observations behind each of the seemingly contradictory value ideologies. The true and correct observations can be surmised by taking each of the ideologies to be based on one of the primary psychological needs that Self-Determination Theory has revealed. The Social Justice ideology is based on the need for relatedness, the Accountability ideology is based on the need for competence, and the Freedom ideology is based on the need for autonomy.

I have told these stories about relativity problems because the change effort I am proposing is, by definition, going to be critical of anything that causes the human needs of some people in the system to be neglected or thwarted. Any given ideology, policy, or practice may not be consistent with actual observations of primary human need supports and

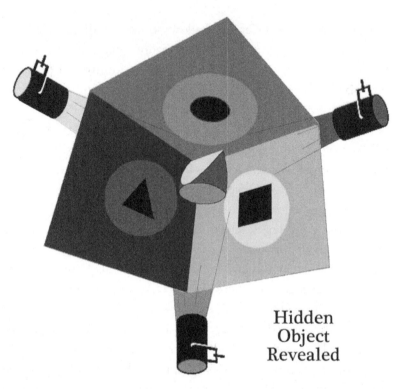

**Hidden
Object
Revealed**

deeper learning. Everyone is going to be both right and wrong. The challenge is to conform to the reality of human needs and deeper learning, not to traditions of ideology, policy, and practice. Teacher-centered or student-centered doesn't matter except to the degree that each of the humans in that situation are having their needs thwarted or supported. For now, we have very limited information about what is working to support human needs and what is not. The point of the Protect, Measure, and Manage provisions of the resolution presented in Chapter 6 are to help us get attuned to the right information to figure it out in each and every unique school context.

Situational Design by Analogy[108]

How will we know when we have achieved equity? An equitable school system should be adequately funded, provide a diverse population

---

[108] This analogy was first presented in my book *Education Can ONLY Be Offered: How K-12 Schools Will Save Democracy* (Berg, 2017) (See References for full citations.)

with appropriate opportunities according to their personal and cultural needs, and respond to the needs of the society, as well. But these are vague generalities; they aren't specific enough to act on.

Another set of criteria for equity is Shariff Abdullah's ideas for describing a world that works for all: Enoughness, Exchangability, and Common Benefit. In the quote below from his book *Creating A World That Works for All* he uses the example of a Sarvodaya canteen in Sri Lanka as an example. Sarvodaya is a large non-profit organization that applies Gandhian peace principles to the economic, political, and social challenges in the island nation.[109]

> It was in the Sarvodaya canteen that I could see a microcosm of a world that worked for all. For Sarvodaya workers and the foreign volunteers that the organization attracts from around the world, the canteen is a meeting place. They gather there for their meals and, twice a day, for supersweet British-style tea. Lunch is the grand confluence, with hundreds of workers, volunteers, and visitors sharing a meal.
>
> In the canteen, foreigners are treated differently from the native Sri Lankans. To summarize the differences:
>
> - Foreigners (visitors and workers) eat from china plates; Sri Lankans eat from wide, shallow bowls made of metal.
>
> - Foreigners get served at a special table reserved for them; Sri Lankans eat at all the other tables.

---

[109] "[T]he Sarvodaya Shramadana Movement (officially known as "Lanka Jathika Sarvodaya Shramadana Sangamaya") is Sri Lanka's most broadly embedded community-based development organization network. Sarvodaya works with 26 district centres, 325 divisional centres and over 3,000 legally independent village societies in districts across the country, including war-torn northern and eastern provinces." Source: https://www.sarvodaya.org/about-us

- Foreigners are served "family style" from platters of food. Generally, they have twice the amount of food available as any human being could possibly eat. (If eating alone, a person is served enough food for two on the platters; a group of six is served enough for twelve.) Sri Lankans get their food by going to the kitchen door, where they are given a plate heaped with rice and all of the same curries that are found on the foreigners' table. If they are still hungry after eating their first serving, they simply go back to the kitchen door for another plate of food.

After observing this system carefully, I came to the conclusion that it provided the best way to serve a large group of people representing different cultures, different gastronomic capacities and tastes, and different eating styles and habits.

Some Westerners, especially Americans who have been through "diversity training," see things differently. They loudly protest the "privileges" of having "more food," china plates, and table service. A few, totally disregarding Sri Lankan culture and courtesy, will try to get food in the kitchen line, which confuses everybody. (Because it is a Sri Lankan custom to offer abundant food and hospitality to guests, the Americans who try to be "culturally correct" will still find a china plate and generous servings waiting for them after they have stood in line for a Sri Lankan plate!) [110]

---

[110] Abdullah, 1999 pp. 18-19

The Sarvodaya Canteen works because of three principles of equity: *Enoughness* means that every person has enough, no one is left out. Despite serving the various people differently according to Sri Lankan customs, everyone gets fed.

Exchangability means that if you exchange places with anyone else in the system you will still be OK, even if you would not prefer to do so. Even the richest and poorest, socially connected and isolated, etc. can switch places and survive; even though some are not likely to desire the switch, they will not unduly suffer or die because of it (where "undue" does not apply to the temporary suffering induced by lifestyle adjustment).

Common Benefit means that the system is designed for the mutual benefit of all participants, even if they do not all receive the same things from it. This means there are no scapegoats. No one within the system is singled out to receive disadvantages, no one gets the short end of the stick merely because someone else happens to dislike an inherent trait they happen to have.

The design principles presented in the Transportation vs. Education Table in chapter 3 are intended to produce equitable outcomes that meet these kind of criteria in the process of addressing the disengagement problem. Viewing equity through a psychological lens suggests to me the third strategic commitment of Back to Basics 2.0: When things get hard, provide more support, not less. The fundamental assumption here is that we are all in this together. If we don't provide support for each other then our actions will predictably lead to the disintegration of the community. Granted, we need to be clear about the limits of the kinds of support that can be provided at each level of the system, but we need to be working toward a system that is pervasively need supportive. It is counter-productive for the large-scale system to eventually write some people off. That kind of callous attitude will eventually come back to bite us in an interconnected global society.

The solution to the most fundamental problem affecting our schools is easy to state but difficult to implement. We just need to get teachers and students more engaged. But, changing large-scale institutions is never simple nor straightforward. The fact is that the institutions we want to affect are complex and adaptive, just like we are. Therefore, the change process needs to be informed by a strategy that is also adaptive. That is the intention behind the resolution process proposed in the next chapter.

7 A POLICY FRAMEWORK FOR HUMAN SYSTEMS OF EDUCATION

Systems Change

This book has, so far, been concerned with ideas and theories about how the system is and how it should be. Now it is time to shift our attention to bridging the gap between what is and what should be in practical terms. For some, the invocation of the term "practical" suggests that I should now tell individuals how to behave better in classrooms and schools. However, that would be an *im*practical strategy because of the fact that classrooms and schools are embodied by and embedded in complex adaptive systems, as noted earlier. Changing individual behaviors as a means of reforming the system is like building a sand castle below the high tide line at the beach and then expecting it to still be there when you return the next day. The policies and organizational habits at the larger levels within the system are a tidal force that regularly resets the behavioral landscape.

Larry Cuban's history of classroom practice, mentioned in Chapter 6, suggests that outstanding enthusiastic behavioral change efforts have popped up repeatedly over the course of the history of schooling, student-centered pedagogy being just one example. Most of these have been washed out, leaving in place the original organizational habits or something close to them over the long term, as indicated by the notable

stability and resistance to change within the school system writ large. The best hope for effective change is to identify or create leverage points at a larger level that can be used to take advantage of windows of opportunity to make changes at the lower levels. At those opportune moments the various actors who have been properly organized and prepared to express a human-centered attitude-first view can make sustainable changes.

It is in the nature of a large-scale dynamic system that there are occasionally moments when something happens to kill off an old habit or to create the possibility of an innovation that can generate new habits. The challenge for large-scale change in education is to have people attuned to the dynamics of organizational and societal change who are prepared to take advantage of opportunities to insert appropriate methods of supporting primary human needs rather than continuously accepting the default of delivering academics in need thwarting ways. The key to preparing the way for this kind of sustained effort is ensuring that there is a pocket of protection within the system for this kind of innovation to withstand the countervailing forces that would wear it away.

The democratic schools I've mentioned previously are examples of self-directed education, but most of them are private schools in which parents pay tuition. However, over the last 100 years there have been some instances of this "radical" pedagogy being in place on the publicly managed side of the school system. These public schools have had to endure repeated challenges to their existence and/or steady pressure to erode the degree of student self-direction they provided. A few examples of democratic schools in the public sphere include Windsor House in Vancouver, BC, Canada (maybe closing or reorganizing in 2019), Trillium Charter School in Portland, OR, USA (closed in 2019), the New Orleans Free School (closed 2005), and Jefferson County Open School in Lakewood, CO, USA. Given the rise and fall of various movements in favor of student self-direction over the last century, there are probably innumerable other examples that have been lost to history. These rare public schools and their perennial challenges provide us with a sense of what we can expect in terms of institutional resistance.

The large-scale and concomitant complexity of the public system has given it a form of resilience that has been likened to an immunity to change. The metaphor is good, but the roles are backwards. What the system-as-body has is a memetic infection that is causing inhumane disengagement on a massive scale. The infectious agent is the idea that education is primarily the making and taking of deliveries (a.k.a. the banking model in which content is deposited into the heads of students by teachers, ala Paulo Friere). What we need to do is give this human system an immune boost that will bring healthy, true education to the fore and manage or cure the memetic infection that is currently causing rampant disengagement.

Boosting the immunity of a human social system has to be explicitly expressed at the policy level at some point in order for the default patterns to be effectively changed over the long term. In a review of the research conducted in mainstream schools on the lack of support for the primary human need for autonomy, psychologist Johnmarshall Reeve pointed out that policy is one of several culprits in this situation.[111] At the policy level there does not seem to be any awareness that primary psychological need support is a necessary input in the school system.

---

[111] Reeve, 2009

Therefore, a new policy framework is needed to enable policy makers to productively alter the situation of mainstream schools by shifting classroom and school practices toward primary human need supports. Satisfaction of primary needs is the input that will lead to intrinsic motivation and engagement. When individuals have their primary needs supported, not only do those individuals show higher intrinsic motivation and engagement, but they also have a greater ability to support others in satisfying their needs.[112] The focus on human need supports will improve the engagement of learners (both students and teachers) and will ultimately result in deeper learning becoming more widespread.

The journalist Andrea Gabor's book *After the Education Wars: How Smart Schools Upend the Business of Reform* is a lengthy exploration of how such mechanisms worked to varying degrees of success in New York City, New Orleans, and Massachusetts between the 1980's and today.[113] She emphasizes how broadly inclusive collaborative change efforts that are highly responsive to local concerns are the most sustainable forms of organizational change, not only in education, but in business, too. While strong leadership is important, it is crucial to understand that leadership needs to be strong at multiple levels in complex organizational systems.

The organizational leaders that need to be influenced the most are, in order of greatest to least leverage in the American public system: legislators, regulators, district board members, district administrators, and school principals. Those leaders are responsible for at least 85% of our children. The most powerful form of support occurs when legislators create special legal designations that specify the kinds of systems and practices that are being protected and targeted for support. In the next level down the power-scale, regulations are made within the jurisdiction of an agency that administers legislated policies. Next are district policies and administration. Finally, there is school policy.

The American private school and quasi-private charter school side of the system is serving less than 12% of all children in the USA (~4-5%

---

[112] Friedman, Deci, Elliot, Moller, & Aarts, 2010; Radel, Sarrazin, Legrain, & Wild, 2010; Reeve, 2009; Taylor, Ntoumanis, & Standage, 2008

[113] Gabor, 2018

are homeschooling). In private schools the hierarchy is usually much shorter, depending on how many schools each school board is responsible for managing. Leadership hierarchies in charter schools can fall just about anywhere in between. Private and quasi-private school leaders may have more flexibility to change their organizations, but very few, if any, of them are well positioned to catalyze changes in the rest of the system. While these schools can serve as valuable proofs of concept, they will need to be given support to become effective system-wide leaders who can influence policies and practices within the much larger public side.

The science should be clear to scientists, and perhaps to practitioners, but to the numerous non-scientists and non-practitioners in those positions of potential leverage the implications need to be made explicit. The practical implications of scientifically well-established theoretical concepts require explicit statement in the policies of our education system. Research on the way political decisions are made suggests that moral and emotional factors are as much or more important than "rational" factors.[114] Organizational leaders should convene locally meaningful policy discussions that can begin to move their organization in the right direction.

Policy makers in the recent past have focused mostly on outputs, not inputs. For instance, Jim Liebman, the former chief accountability officer for New York City public schools, once said, "We believe it's not about inputs, it's about outcomes."[115] When policy makers did put their focus on inputs they usually paid attention to the wrong ones. They acted as if teachers just need to be held more accountable for the instructional inputs and the academic outcomes. This is understandable because they are not tracking the leading edges of psychological research and cannot be expected to have realized that there is a whole realm of non-academic and non-instructional inputs that they have to be responsible for providing.

---

[114] Greene, 2013; Haidt, 2007, 2012; Stone, et al., 2014; see Hanson & Yosifon, 2003, for a well-developed argument against assumptions of "rationality"

[115] Fertig, 2009 p. 285

The system should be focused on creating pervasive primary human need support. The system-level architects, designers, builders, managers, and maintainers (e.g. policy makers, board members, administrators, principals, etc.) should be fully cognizant of this while the front line users (e.g. teachers and students) should be able to generally ignore it in their run-of-the-mill day-to-day experiences. The dynamics of managing the large-scale patterns within school organizations is just as much a specialized technical arena as any other advanced subject, like computer programming. In the same way that most children and teachers use computers, but few have an interest in programming, children and teachers will be users of the education system. It is unrealistic to expect more than a few to take an interest in the management challenges. Students should be able to focus on their educational and learning goals (either finding or pursuing them) and whatever healthy human aspirations they and their families have. All students should be offered but not forced into accepting opportunities to get good feedback about reality from reality itself, ideally, but from teachers and other members of their community when that is not safe, not practical, or is otherwise unavailable. The students should be invited to make meaningful contributions to their communities in order to demonstrate what they have been learning.[116] As the challenges of data security at companies like Facebook and Google have demonstrated, the system's leaders need to be responsive to the concerns that users will naturally have about the moral directions the system is going. Leaders need to take the issue of being entrusted with great power seriously and ensure that they are steering the system in a respectful, responsible, and resourceful direction in which primary needs are universally supported. To help them with that task I present a resolution below that can be used as the center piece of a reform campaign.

---

[116] Consistent with best practices found in schools that claim to be aiming for deeper learning (Bogle, 2016).

Why propose a resolution, not a binding law?[117]

I am educated as a motivation psychologist, not a law maker. I conclude from the science that there are primary human needs, but it does not follow that imposing a universal legal mandate to support those needs would or could be effective. While the needs apply to all humans, how they are culturally expressed and organizationally supported varies. It would be antithetical to the support of the primary human need for autonomy to make a universal imposition that is insensitive to local circumstances and cultural variations.

Ultimately, success in getting this policy proposal enacted requires the engagement of politicians and other leaders in the legislative and policy making processes. Politicians are human; therefore the logical application of the scientific conclusion suggests that we support the autonomy of the politicians (and other human leaders), rather than attempt to exert control over them. I, therefore, offer the benefit of my expertise in the theory of human needs and how it applies in education generally, but ask them to be the experts in composing context-sensitive laws and policies.

Policy makers should work with motivation psychologists to ensure that the laws they compose appropriately honor the needs of all the humans subjected to them. Their participation in the process of interacting with experts is also likely to enable them to grow a deeper understanding of the issues. Deeper understanding will help them communicate strategically about the practical challenges. Their ability to communicate effectively will help build appropriate support for passing those laws in their unique community context. I cannot possibly write a policy that could accurately anticipate all the contextual variations of my audiences, so I modestly propose a resolution that can be used by political experts as a foundation for appropriate laws and policies.

The Resolution

The resolution begins with a moral assertion about nurturing, where nurturing is defined as support of primary human needs. This is an

---

[117] I thank Kayla Good for her assistance with the research for this resolution and its original presentation at the 5th International Self-Determination Theory Conference in 2016.

unusual way to begin a resolution. The resolution is a method of framing the decisions of school leaders in terms that are grounded more deeply than those of partisan ideology. Cognitive linguistic research and analysis suggests that nurturing is universally regarded as a fundamental moral obligation of families.[118] Through the ubiquitous Nation-As-Family metaphor for implicitly conceptualizing politics, what distinguishes the worldviews of liberals from that of conservatives is the ways that nurturing is ideally supposed to be expressed by parents.[119] Both sides accept that nurturing is a duty of parenting; what differs is how to express nurturing. According to linguist George Lakoff, when politics is conceived of in terms of this metaphor the two sides differentiate themselves along ideological lines that make sense only in terms of the metaphor. If schools are conceived of as an extension of family concerns, then the moral obligation to nurture children applies. The State is not considered to be normally nor naturally implicated in nurturing, but to the degree that the State has an interest in the well-being of its citizens, then logically it must take responsibility for ensuring that their primary human needs are supported. This is especially true of citizens who happen to be children, thus both parents and the State have the same obligation for nurturing when children are involved.

After establishing this moral mandate for the proposed policy we proceed with more traditional assertions of fact that are either empirically supported or logically related to the empirical findings. The conclusions are focused on 1) encouraging and supporting primary need support and 2) guiding practical policy interventions that would drive organizational members to ever more consistently enact need supportive behaviors.

The "Primary Need Support Is The Foundation of Deeper Learning" Resolution

Preamble: Deeper learning is required to understand and productively contribute to our globalized society. Deeper learning

---

[118] Lakoff, 1996, 2008; Lakoff & Johnson, 1999

[119] Lakoff, 1996, 2008; Lakoff & Johnson, 1999

depends on engagement; unfortunately, evidence shows that the majority of K-12 students and teachers are disengaged. But students and teachers are not the ultimate cause of this problem; the problem is caused by many decades of policies and school leadership that have systematically discouraged adults and children from enacting need supportive behaviors in schools. A lack of need support leads to disengagement. This policy framework will help guide policy makers and school leaders to enable and encourage need support instead.

Moral Mandate

WHEREAS, all adults responsible for children must nurture them.[120]

Findings of Fact

Nurturing Defined

WHEREAS, nurturing, in this context, means supporting a person (of any age) to satisfy their primary human needs.[121]

---

[120] According to Lakoff & Johnson (1999), cognitive linguistic research shows that nurturing is one of the experiential foundations of moral reasoning. Thus, the moral mandate above is reasoned to be resonant with most, perhaps all, conceptions of morality independent of more specific partisan positions that may define the sides taken in educational politics. Explicitly activating this moral conception is intended to evoke more positive and proactive responses to the empirical findings that follow and to the policy implications spelled out after that. The moral and practical integrity of the framework primarily depends upon the Measure, Manage, and Protect provisions.

Empirical research suggests that political decision making is guided by emotional and moral sensibilities as much as, and perhaps more than, rational evaluation (Greene, 2013; Haidt, 2007, 2012; see Stone, et al., 2014, for a review of political decision making research). The mandate above is taken to be the self-evidently true moral landscape in which we are situated when setting K-12 educational policy. The rest of the statements of fact following this one clarify the meaning of this moral obligation in the context of K-12 schooling. According to Clifford, Jerit, Rainey, and Motyl (2015), 'Through their appeal to specific moral foundations, elites are able to "moralize" political issues, facilitating (and reinforcing) the connection between people's moral beliefs and their policy attitudes.' They further suggested that targeting the particular moral foundations endorsed by opposing sides of an issue will encourage consensus among people with differing moral beliefs.

[121] This is a definition that narrows the meaning of 'nurturing' to the manageable scope of primary human need support. There may be other aspects of nurturing that are important in

Need Thwarting and Supporting are Contagious

WHEREAS, people whose primary needs are being thwarted are less able to support others to satisfy their primary needs and people whose primary needs are being supported are more able to support others to satisfy their primary needs. (For this reason, in an airplane emergency at high altitude, a parent is required to put on their oxygen mask before putting one on their child.)[122]

What Counts as a Primary Need

WHEREAS, primary needs are universal to all humans, are not derived from any other needs, and have non-neutral effects on well-being.[123]

The Primary Needs

WHEREAS, air, water, food, shelter, sleep, relatedness, autonomy, and competence have been shown to be primary needs (as established by peer-reviewed scientific studies published in widely respected journals).[124]

---

other contexts, but this definition is intended for use in schools. This narrow technical definition can help prevent unduly privileging the cultural or idiosyncratic variations in meaning that inevitably arise when the term 'nurturing' is used in an everyday colloquial sense.

[122] The parenthetical reference to airplane emergencies is an important framing for the challenge that school leaders face. Need support is dependent on multiple levels of influence, including societal expectations (Reeve, 2009). Studies show that motivation is contagious and that the level of need support teachers receive has an effect on the level of need support they will provide to their students (Friedman, Deci, Elliot, Moller, & Aarts, 2010; Radel, Sarrazin, Legrain, & Wild, 2010; Reeve, 2009; Taylor, Ntoumanis, & Standage, 2008).

[123] This is a definition that uses the earliest criteria that were developed within the Self-Determination Theory research tradition to establish which needs should be considered primary and, by logical extension, when other needs would be considered derivative or secondary. Other criteria have been added, but the elaboration of an exhaustive list does not seem necessary in this context.

[124] The needs for oxygen (air), water, material nutrients (food), protection from extreme environmental conditions (shelter), and sleep are taken to be generally accepted as primary. The evidence for the primary psychological needs for relatedness, autonomy, and competence have been established by peer-reviewed scientific studies published in widely respected journals (Deci & Ryan, 2000, 2012; Ryan & Deci, 2000a, 2006; Sheldon, Ryan, & Reis, 1996). They have received empirical support in both adult (Baard, Deci, & Ryan, 2004; Reis, Sheldon, Gable, Roscoe, & Ryan, 2000) and child populations (Veronneau, Koestner, & Abela, 2005). Cross

(But, NOT Maslow!)

(WHEREAS, 'Maslow's Hierarchy of Needs,' despite being intuitively compelling and gaining widespread fame, is a mixture of primary and derivative needs and it fails to provide a useful model for the present purpose.)[125]

Un-Met Needs = Poor Health

WHEREAS, thwarting the needs for relatedness, autonomy, and competence leads to anxiety, depression, and other forms of psychological distress.[126]

Mental Ill-being Defined

WHEREAS, anxiety, depression, and other forms of psychological distress are forms of mental ill-being.

---

cultural studies covering Belgium, Bulgaria, China, Japan, USA, Peru, Russia, South Korea, and Turkey support the case for the universality of those primary psychological needs (Chen, Beiwen, Vansteenkiste, Beyers, Boone, Deci, Van Der Kaap-Deeder, Duriez, et al., 2015; Chirkov, Ryan, Kim, & Kaplan, 2003; Deci, Ryan, Gagne, Leona, Usunov, & Kornazheva, 2001; Nishimura & Takashi, 2016; Chirkov, 2009 argues for the universality of autonomy specifically).

[125] Even with the most generous interpretation of the scientific literature, either Maslow's Hierarchy is wrong or it is irrelevant to this resolution. For instance, a spirited defense of Maslow was undertaken recently by Taormina & Gao (2013). The researchers addressed many of the fundamental criticisms that were levelled in previous studies and reviews of the literature. One of the main contributions of this study was to more precisely define the elements of Maslow's Hierarchy in terms of deficits. This re-interpretation means that the intuitive appeal of Maslow's Hierarchy is explained by the mix of derivative and primary needs in the elements of the model. The elements that are not already included in the list of primary needs represent motives. This reframing from needs to motives renders Maslow's model non-foundational from the perspective of this resolution and, therefore, irrelevant to the current purpose. A sample of Maslow related research, reviews, and modification proposals were reviewed to assess its potential to inform this resolution (Kenrick, Griskevicius, Neuberg, & Schaller, 2010; Littrell, 2012, Ryan, & Deci, 2000b; Taormina, & Gao, 2013; Tay, & Diener, 2011; Wahba, & Bridwel, 1976).

[126] A variety of studies have looked at various relationships between the primary psychological needs and other indicators of well-/ill-being and generally confirmed the negative effects of unmet needs (Baard, Deci, & Ryan, 2004; Deci, & Ryan, 1985, 2012; Hodgins, & Liebeskind, 2003; Hodgins, Liebeskind, & Schwartz, 1996; Kasser & Ryan, 1993; Nishimura & Takashi, 2016; Ryan, & Connell, 1989).

Poor Health = Less & Worse Learning

WHEREAS, ill-being, whether physical or mental, leads to diminished capacity for learning.[127]

Met Needs = Good Health

WHEREAS, supporting people to meet their needs for relatedness, autonomy, and competence leads to intrinsic motivation and more engagement.[128]

Good Health = More & Better Learning

WHEREAS, intrinsic motivation and engagement lead to optimal learning and the best possible learning outcomes.[129]

---

[127] This is both a logical inference from the other findings of fact and is also a statement of common sense that researchers endorse (Deci & Ryan, 2012). For example, Gottfried (1985) showed that academic anxiety is negatively associated with intrinsic motivation, which is positively correlated with academic achievement.

[128] A variety of studies and literature reviews have examined the relationships between the primary psychological needs, motivation, and engagement (Baard, Deci, & Ryan, 2004; Deci, & Ryan, 2000, 2012; Ryan & Deci, 2000a; Dupont, Galand, Nils, & Hospel, 2014; Ryan & Deci, 2006). Satisfaction of needs for autonomy, competence, and relatedness each positively correlate with positive outcomes for growth and health (specifically, work performance and psychological adjustment), and overall primary needs satisfaction also positively predicts these outcomes (Baard, Deci, & Ryan, 2004). Primary need satisfaction is associated with well-being (e.g., improved mental health, Ryan & Deci, 2000b). According to Schüler, Brandstätter, & Sheldon (2012), 'There is no well-being and flow without need satisfaction [in reference to the need for competence].'

[129] Intrinsic motivation is associated with adaptive coping strategies (Boggiano, 1998; Ryan & Connell, 1989), deep conceptual learning strategies (Meece, Blumenfeld, & Hoyle, 1988; Pintrich & Garcia, 1991), engagement in classroom activities (Otis, Grouzet, & Pelletier, 2005; Ryan & Connell, 1989), positive affect (Gottfried, 1985; Harter, 1981; Harter, et al., 1992; Ryan & Deci, 2000b), and creativity (Amabile, 1996). Intrinsic motivation is also positively associated with academic achievement, favorable perception of academic competence, and minimal academic anxiety (Corpus, Mcclintic-Gilbert, & Hayenga, 2009; Gottfried, Fleming & Gottfried, 2001; Lepper, Corpus, & Iyengar, 2005; for a summary, see Sansone & Harackiewicz, 2007; Stipek, 2002). The more controlled forms of extrinsic motivation, by contrast, are associated with the diminishment of well-being and learning (Assor, Roth, & Deci, 2004; Assor, Kaplan, Kanat-Maymon, & Roth, 2005; Deci & Ryan, 2000; Ryan & Deci, 2000b, 2006).

Intrinsic motivation is positively correlated with grades, while extrinsic motivation is negatively

Self-directed Learning Appears to be Need Supportive

WHEREAS, the maintenance of intrinsic motivation or engagement has been observed (as presented in peer-reviewed scientific studies of student populations published in widely respected journals) only in schools that make academic instruction optional, not mandatory.[130]

Policy Direction

Primary Need Support is the Foundation of Deeper Learning

Therefore, we RESOLVE to recognize that primary need support is fundamental to well-being and must be a non-negotiable input for education because it is the foundation upon which deeper learning is built.

---

correlated with them (Lepper, Corpus, & Iyengar, 2005). Fostering intrinsic motivation in the classroom can facilitate a mastery goal orientation, which is associated with higher classroom engagement as well as enhanced performance on tests (Meece, Blumenfeld, & Hoyle, 1988). Compared to those with an extrinsic orientation, children with an intrinsic orientation improve their strategies when faced with failure, show more internal attributions, greater perceived competence, and more intrinsic orientations after one year (Boggiano, 1998).

According to Early, Rogge, & Deci (2014) in a literature review setting the context for a recent study:

Engagement ... is a prerequisite for school success. It is manifested as effort and persistence and allows students to profit from challenging curricula ... . Many studies published in the past 40 years have confirmed that students who are high in intrinsic motivation are more engaged in learning that is deeper and more conceptual ... and perform better on heuristic, as opposed to algorithmic, tasks ... . There is also evidence that when students have fully internalized the regulation for learning, they tend to be more engaged in learning and to perform better than when learning is controlled by external contingencies ... .

[130] Intrinsic motivation and engagement were shown to be maintained amongst students who were being homeschooled, attending democratic schools, or attending EdVisions Charter Schools (Berg & Corpus, 2013; Van Ryzin, Gravely, & Roseth, 2009; Van Ryzin, 2011; Vedder-Weiss, & Fortus, 2010). Autonomy-supportive teaching and provision of structure are associated with higher student engagement (Jang, Reeve, & Deci, 2010) and higher intrinsic motivation (Koestner, Ryan, Bernieri, & Holt, 1984). There is evidence to suggest that the decline in intrinsic motivation found across grade levels (i.e., as students age) in 'traditional' schools is not significant amongst homeschooled students or students attending a democratic school. (Berg & Corpus, 2013) (Note that other schools, especially those who espouse deeper learning as an aspiration, may also maintain intrinsic motivation and engagement, but evidence has not yet been published in peer-reviewed journals.)

Primary Need Support is a Duty of Leadership
Therefore, we RESOLVE to recognize that primary need support is a pervasive responsibility of all adults in organizations that serve children of any age and also a responsibility of all leaders with power over other people.

Everyone Must Have Their Primary Needs Supported
Therefore, we RESOLVE to recognize that both adults and children must have their primary needs supported in order for organizations serving children to be effective and efficient educational organizations.

Primary Need Support Precedes Pedagogy
Therefore, we RESOLVE to support primary needs as a necessary precondition for deeper learning and as a logical precedent to all the various purposes of education that deeper learning will serve, the instructional choices that follow from those purposes, and the implementation of those instructional choices.

Need Support Precedes Valued Outcomes
Therefore, we RESOLVE to safeguard primary need support by giving it functional precedence over the pursuit of other valuable educational goals such as possessing basic or advanced knowledge and skills, job readiness, and preparation for college.[131]

Measure
Therefore, we RESOLVE to assess organizational climate at least twice per year using an instrument that includes measures of psychological well-being and that has been validated through peer-reviewed scientific research (e.g. the Hope Survey).

---

[131] The term 'functional' is used here in order to contrast it with rhetorical precedence. A school might promote itself in a manner that suggests they prioritize something else above all other considerations. As long as the prioritization of primary need support reflects its role as a non-negotiable input as demonstrated by the Measure, Manage, and Protect provisions that follow, then there is no cause for concern over whatever rhetorical flourishes a school uses to promote itself.

Manage

Therefore, we RESOLVE to establish a pattern of climate data demonstrating that the people within our organization maintain their intrinsic motivation and/or engagement for the typical activities they do.

Protect

Therefore, we RESOLVE to protect the features of our organization that have been shown to be causally related to the support of primary needs, intrinsic motivation, or engagement.

The intention here is to provide a framework for inserting nurturing (as defined) into the system at every possible opportunity. This change process requires the front line people to be paying attention to what changes are being offered up and shaping the dialogue about each proposed change with these ideas in mind. By constantly raising the issues of primary need support, that idea can become an integral part of how the institution makes changes. By taking the small (seemingly ineffectual) step of passing a resolution, we create a new method for organizational activists to justify an on-going insistence on raising key issues of need support, motivation, and engagement that are, in fact, central to human learning. Correcting institutional patterns will require sustained efforts over a long time because these issues have traditionally been neglected due to the delusion that education primarily consists of delivering knowledge. The resolution will be effective if there is enough follow-up that would make the assertions of policy direction into regular, on-going dialogues that subsequently shape binding laws, policies, and organizational habits.

In order to get a more practical handle on this particular mode of change through a resolution, we look to a recent campaign and the lessons drawn from it by some of its leaders. The Portland Public School Board here in Oregon passed a resolution regarding climate justice. Bill Bigelow and Tim Swinehart wrote a reflection on the lessons that they learned as leaders along the way. Just one of their items had to be adapted to fit the specific agenda we are pursuing here, the rest hold true, independent of the content of the resolution. These lessons make it clear that sustained success is dependent on sustained engagement. Policies delivered as directive communication from a board can sometimes be mistaken for magical spells with miraculous powers to change human and organizational behavior. A miraculous change may be possible, but it will require sustained hard work before the result can ever be considered for the status of a miracle.

Nine Organizing Lessons From A Successful Resolution Campaign[132]

- Start broad, go slow, involve educators and non-educators
- Draft a quality resolution
- Argue for primary need support, not just against disengagement (adapted item)
- Build support before going public
- Seek support from sympathetic school board members
- Make the school board consideration of the resolution a community event
- Have a media strategy; be prepared for criticism
- Solidify your base after passage
- Think about implementation from early in the process.

As you begin to put together a team and a plan I encourage you to consider taking a trans-partisan approach to the challenge. This suggestion will inform how you tackle the fourth and the seventh lessons above, building support before going public and having a media strategy that anticipates criticism. In order to achieve trans-partisanship you will need to have representatives of a variety of positions on education issues recruited into the campaign before going public.

---

[132] Bigelow, 2016

CONCLUSION:
IMPLEMENTING BACK TO BASICS 2.0

In our school system we need to be clear that the necessary output is educated citizens who have had consistent access to deeper learning; this will inherently empower citizens to become more engaged and effective members of society. The reality of learning is such that this goal can only be achieved if we produce the right conditions for deeper learning in our schools. Producing those conditions requires that we pay attention to and provide support for primary human needs, with emphasis on the psychological ones. When we neglect or, worse, thwart needs, then the humans involved (students, teachers, etc.) become psychologically distressed; this shows up as anxiety, depression, and other symptoms. Psychological distress prevents deeper learning.

Our existing school system was designed without benefit of the idea of primary human needs, but it should not continue to ignore them. We can look to the psychological research tradition of Self-Determination Theory for ways to develop better feedback about the psychological conditions in schools.[133] Within that research community there are a variety of measures that assess need supports, need satisfaction, motivation, and engagement. Establishing systematic feedback will require us to look first at patterns of engagement. Gallup's Student Poll

---

[133] Deci & Ryan, 1985, 2000; Ryan & Deci, 2000a, 2000b (See References for full citations.)

is an excellent and free resource that most schools in the USA can take advantage of fairly quickly. Assessment of the other psychological aspects will need to be handled more locally in order to be sensitive to the contextual factors that influence how each individual is experiencing the school setting. The Hope Survey is an instrument that has been used successfully in some schools in the USA and has peer-reviewed evidence to suggest that it provides valuable feedback.[134] The various other measures within Self-Determination Theory have mostly been developed for pure research and will likely need to be adapted and supported in order to better meet the needs of school practitioners and managers. Next steps should also include ensuring that this new strategy of supporting and assessing human needs is implemented globally.

The deep disconnect between K-12 schooling and psychology is due to an emerging paradigm shift in the conception of human nature. Today the dominant conception of learning that is informing mainstream schools is the delivery of content about a knowable universe from one atomic self into another. The content delivery conception of learning and the human nature required in order to for it to succeed are nonsensical from the perspective of current psychological science. However, there is an emerging conception of human nature that takes the fact that we are embedded in and embodied by systems to mean that our interaction with the world is deeply informed by our primary human needs, even though we don't consciously realize it. We humans are all capable of amazing feats of adaptivity that are incredibly sensitive to the subtleties and nuances of our situations, but such accomplishments depend on systematic primary need satisfaction.

The kind of learning that is necessary to adaptively deal with our complex global society today requires that our primary needs be supported. By putting need supports in place and managing the system according to feedback that monitors and modifies the patterns of engagement, we can expect that both learners and teachers will be better able to adaptively adjust their behavior to the situations in which they find themselves. It is not helpful at the systems level to think about skills

---

[134] Newell & Van Ryzin, 2009; Van Ryzin, Gravelly, & Roseth, 2009; Van Ryzin, 2011

and traits (though it may be at the classroom level); it is more helpful to think about the determinants of deeper learning, like patterns of engagement (or attitude). There are lots of other things we need to think about and manage, but addressing the engagement problem is going to make all our other educational challenges a lot easier to deal with. When deeper learning becomes the norm rather than the exception we will have far more productive and creative human resources available to tackle our other problems.

Ultimately our global society needs good citizens. Most people would like to be good citizens and expect help to achieve that outcome from their governing institutions, starting with their childhood family and extending to all state and non-state organizations to which they belong. Good citizenship requires deeper learning, regardless of where or with whom each citizen resides. Deeper learning requires primary human needs to be supported. We did not previously realize that the psychological needs for autonomy, competence, and relatedness were primary. Now that we know better, we can start to reorganize our school system to pay attention to the psychological conditions in schools. Collecting and analyzing data about the psychological conditions in schools in order to create conditions that support deeper learning should be a foundational piece of school reform agendas, regardless of political affiliations. Once we automatically and systematically recognize how absurd it is to thwart those needs, we will have turned the corner away from doing inadvertent systematic harm towards creating a system that reliably facilitates deeper learning for *all students.*

We need to get back to basics but we need to replace the old version. Back to basics v2.0 requires three things of school leaders:
1. Teach governance before academics.
2. Manage for engagement, not obedience.
3. When things get hard, provide more support, not less.

When we inspire more joy we will reveal more genius. Systematically revealing more genius will make K-12 into a system of enthusiastic students taught by passionate teachers in joyful schools.

Back to Basics 1.0

1. 3R's of Academics
Reading, 'Riting, & 'Rithmetic

2. No Nonsense in the Classroom
No frivolous activities

3. Strict Discipline
Teachers assert authority and children obey

Result: ~70% Disengagement
Disengagement = Shallow Learning

Back to Basics 2.0

1. Teach Governance Before Academics
More democracy, less dictatorship

2. Manage for Engagement
Provide activities that lead to deeper learning, not boredom

3. When it gets hard, provide more support, not less
Supporting primary human needs leads to better citizenship

Be human before being academic!

APPENDIX: DEEPER LEARNING ADVOCATES

The following is a summary of the premises and aims of Deeper Learning Advocates, the organization that I lead. We are a membership organization devoted to bring about the political changes necessary for transforming the education system to better meet the needs of students and teachers.

A Quick Outline of the Learning Problem

Common Sense

- Good citizenship requires education
- Schools are necessary (even though education happens outside of schools, too)
- Today, deep learning is required to become educated
  - Institutional patterns that consistently diminish the depth of learning are <u>intolerable expedients</u>
  - <u>Intolerable expedients</u> include:
    - suffocation, dehydration, starvation, & exposure (thwarting primary *physiological* needs)
    - sleep deprivation (thwarting a primary *psychological* need)

- o The existence of <u>intolerable expedients</u> in our K-12 school system is caused by a combination of historical accidents and ignorance of recent scientific insights into learning.

  - ▪ Mainstream K-12 school management currently emphasizes <u>obedience</u> over **engagement**

Recent Scientific Insights Into Learning

- **Engagement** is a prerequisite for deep learning

  - o **Engagement** naturally follows from the satisfaction of primary human needs

    - ▪ When <u>obedience</u> undermines primary human needs it can cause **disengagement**

  - o <u>Intolerable expedients</u> include thwarting primary *psychological* needs for autonomy, competence, & relatedness

    - ▪ Management for <u>obedience</u> via <u>intolerable expedients</u> causes rampant **disengagement** resulting in a global problem that Gallup estimates is costing us $7 trillion per year.

- Evidence suggests that family-directed and self-directed learning situations are at least as good as mainstream K-12 schooling (teacher- and school-directed learning situations) on traditional metrics, but superior on **engagement** metrics

Deeper Learning Advocates is championing a new strategy to solve this $7 trillion global learning problem, but we need your help to pull it off.

Bottom line

<u>Manage for engagement, not obedience.</u>

Vision:

We envision enthusiastic students being taught by passionate teachers in joyful K-12 schools that are managed for engagement, not obedience.

Mission:

We assist school leaders with embedding the psychology of learning in policy so that policy will stop undermining learning.

Strategy:

Sustainable organizational climate change requires top-down protection for bottom-up innovation. Policy makers can create new opportunities for innovation by enacting the "Primary Needs are the Foundation of Deeper Learning" Resolution (presented in Chapter 6 of this book) and putting aside money to support their front-line staff and faculty to create or adopt innovations that are aligned with the psychology of learning. Resolutions are not legally binding, but they are strong signals to the rest of the organization that the leaders are pointing everyone in a new direction. Part of the deal is that the leaders forego academic data until there is robust psychological climate data revealing the patterns of motivation and engagement that are at the core of deeper learning. During the planning and approval process innovators identify the status quo policies (such as academic data requirements or any other onerous impositions) that erode their ability to enact or maintain their particular innovation. The policy makers would then pass legally binding policies that would ensure that the innovators get enough time (5-10 years for whole school changes) and resources to act on their proposal as long as they are showing that they are improving or maintaining the motivation and engagement of students and teachers.

Action Plan:

#1 Make the case for deeper learning policy campaigns in this book

#2 Recruit individuals and organizations to join as monthly contributing members

#3 Catalyze & support deeper learning policy campaigns throughout the K-12 industry

Help us advocate for better K-12 schools—join today!

DLAdvocates.org

Join DLA

REFERENCES

Abdullah, S., (1999) *Creating a world that works for all.* San Francisco, CA: Berrett-Koehler Publishers, Inc.

AEE (Alliance for Excellent Education). "What about deeper learning." Deeper Learning. Accessed May 18, 2017. http://deeperlearning4all.org/about-deeper-learning.

AINCSEAD (Aspen Institute National Commission on Social, Emotional, & Academic Development, The). (2018). *From A Nation At Risk To A Nation At Hope- Recommendations from the National Commission on Social, Emotional, & Academic Development* (Rep.). Washington, DC: The Aspen Institute.

Amabile, T. (1996). *Creativity in context: update to The social psychology of creativity.* Boulder, Co: Westview Press.

Ariely, D. (2008). *Predictably irrational: the hidden forces that shape our decisions.* New York, NY: HarperCollins.

Assor, A., Kaplan, H., Kanat-Maymon, Y., & Roth, G. (2005). Directly controlling teacher behaviors as predictors of poor motivation and engagement in girls and boys: The role of anger and anxiety. *Learning and Instruction*, 15(5), 397-413. doi:10.1016/j.learninstruc.2005.07.008

Assor, A., Roth, G., & Deci, E. L. (2004). The emotional costs of parents' conditional regard: A self-determination theory analysis. *Journal of Personality*, 72(1), 47-88.

Ayduk, O. (2007). Delay of Gratification in Children: Contributions to Social-Personality Psychology. In Y. Shoda, D. Cervone, & G. Downey (Eds.), *Persons In Context: Building a Science of the Individual* (pp. 97-109). New York, NY: Guilford Press.

Baard, P.P., Deci, E.L., & Ryan, R.M. (2004). Intrinsic need satisfaction: A motivational basis of performance and well-being in two work settings. *Journal of Applied Social Psychology, 34*(10), 2045–2068. DOI: 10.1111/j.1559-1816.2004.tb02690.x

Bao, X., & Lam, S. (2008). Who makes the choice? Rethinking the role of autonomy and relatedness in Chinese children's motivation. *Child Development, 79*(2), 269-283. DOI: 10.1111/j.1467-8624.2007.01125.x

Bellanca, J.A. (Ed.). (2015). *Deeper learning: beyond 21st century skills.* Bloomington, IN: Solution Tree Press. ISBN 978-1-936763-35-1

Berg, D., (2017) *Education Can ONLY Be Offered: How K-12 Schools Will Save Democracy.* Portland, OR: Attitutor Media. ISBN 978-0-9994888-0-5

Berg, D., Allen, H., (2015) *Most Schools Won't Fit.* Portland, OR: Attitutor Media. ISBN 978-0-9994888-1-2

Berg, D., Corpus, J.H., (2013) Enthusiastic Students: A Study of Motivation in Two Alternatives to Mandatory Instruction. *Other Education, 2*(2), 42-66.

Berry, B. (2016) Teacher leadership & deeper learning for all students. (Rep.) Carrboro: Center for Teaching Quality. Print. from https://www.teachingquality.org/deeperlearning

Bigelow, B. (2016). *Organizing Lessons From The Portland Climate Justice Resolution* (Rep.). Portland, OR: Rethinking Schools. Retrieved August 07, 2018, from https://www.rethinkingschools.org/static/publication/apcekit/RS_Portland-Climate-Resolution-Lessons.pdf

Bloom, B. (1984). The Two Sigma Problem: The Search for Methods of Group Instruction as Effective as One-to-one Tutoring. *Educational Researcher,13*(6), 4-16. doi:10.2307/1175554

Boggiano, A.K. (1998). Maladaptive achievement patterns: A test of a diathesis- stress analysis of helplessness. *Journal of Personality and Social Psychology, 74*(6):1681-95. doi: 10.1037//0022-3514.74.6.1681

Bogle, L. (2016, November 03). Study of Deeper Learning: Opportunities and Outcomes. American Institutes of Research. Retrieved from https://www.air.org/project/study-deeper-learning-opportunities-and-outcomes

Bouffard, T., Marcoux, M., Vezeau, C., & Bordeleau, L. (2003). Changes in self-perceptions of competence and intrinsic motivation among elementary school children. *British Journal of Educational Psychology, 73*, 171-186.

Bourne, M. (2014, January 10). We Didn't Eat the Marshmallow. The Marshmallow Ate Us. *New York Times Magazine* Retrieved February 24, 2018, from https://www.nytimes.com/2014/01/12/magazine/we-didnt-eat-the-marshmallow-the-marshmallow-ate-us.html

Bower, G. H. (2007). The Trait versus Situation Debate: A Minimalist View. In Y. Shoda, D. Cervone, & G. Downey (Eds.), *Persons In Context: Building a Science of the Individual* (pp. 19-42). New York, NY: Guilford Press.

Brodinsky, B. (1977). *Defining the Basics of American Education*. Bloomington, IN: Phi Delta Kappa.

Caplan, B. D. (2018). *The case against education: Why the education system is a waste of time and money*. Princeton, NJ: Princeton University Press.

Chen, B., Vansteenkiste, M., Beyers, W., Boone, L., Deci, E. L., Van Der Kaap-Deeder, J., . . . Verstuyf, J. (2015). Basic psychological need satisfaction, need frustration, and need strength across four cultures. *Motivation and Emotion, 39*(2), 216-236. doi: https://doi.org/10.1007/s11031-014-9450-1

Chen, X. (2016). *Remedial Coursetaking at U.S. Public 2- and 4-Year Institutions: Scope, Experiences, and Outcomes* (NCES 2016-405). U.S. Department of Education. Washington, DC: National Center for Education Statistics. Retrieved February 24, 2018, from https://nces.ed.gov/pubs2016/2016405.pdf

Chirkov, V., Ryan, R.M., Kim, Y., & Kaplan, U. (2003). Differentiating autonomy from individualism and independence: A self-determination theory perspective on internalization of cultural orientations and well-being. *Journal of Personality and Social Psychology, 84*(1), 97-110. doi: 10.1037/0022-3514.84.1.97

Chirkov, V.I. (2009) "A cross-cultural analysis of autonomy in education: A self-determination theory perspective." *Theory and Research in Education 7*(2), 253-62. doi: 10.1177/1477878509104330.

Clifford, S., Jerit, J., Rainey, C., & Motyl, M. (2015). Moral Concerns and Policy Attitudes: Investigating the Influence of Elite Rhetoric. *Political Communication, 32*(2), 229–248. doi: http://doi.org/10.1080/10584609.2014.944320

Corpus, J.H., McClintic-Gilbert, M.S., & Hayenga, A.O. (2009). Within-year changes in children's intrinsic and extrinsic motivational orientations: Contextual predictors and academic outcomes. *Contemporary Educational Psychology, 34*(2):154-166. doi: 10.1016/j.cedpsych.2009.01.001

Cuban, L., (1993). *How Teacher's Taught: Constancy and Change in American Classrooms 1890-1990, Second Edition.* New York, NY: Teacher's College Press. ISBN 0-8077-3226-5

Csikszentmihalyi, M. (2001). *Flow: The psychology of optimal experience.* New York, NY: Harper Perennial.

Damasio, A. (2010). *Self Comes to Mind: Constructing the Conscious Brain.* New York, NY: Pantheon Books.

Deci, E. L., & Ryan, R. M. (1980). Self-determination Theory: When Mind Mediates Behavior. *The Journal of Mind and Behavior, 1*(1), 33-43. Retrieved February 7, 2019, from https://www.jstor.org/stable/43852807.

Deci, E. L., & Ryan, R. M. (1985). *Intrinsic motivation and self-determination in human behavior.* New York, NY: Plenum.

Deci, E.L., & Ryan, R.M. (2000). The "what" and "why" of goal pursuits: Human needs and the self-determination of behavior. *Psychological Inquiry,* 11(4), 227-268.

Deci, E.L., & Ryan, R.M. (2012) "Motivation, personality, and development within embedded social contexts: An overview of self-determination theory." In *Oxford handbook of human motivation,* edited by Richard M. Ryan, 85-107. Oxford, UK: Oxford University Press. doi: 10.1093/oxfordhb/9780195399820.001.0001

Deci, E.L., Ryan, R.M., Gagne, M., Leona, D. R., Usunov, J., & Kornazheva, B. P. (2001). Need satisfaction, motivation, and well-being in the work organizations of a former eastern bloc country: A cross-cultural study of self-determination. *Personality & Social Psychology Bulletin 27*(8), 930-942. doi: http://dx.doi.org/10.1177/0146167201278002

Degenaar, J. (2013). Through the inverting glass: first-person observations on spatial vision and imagery. *Phenomenology and the Cognitive Sciences, 13*(2), 373-393. doi:10.1007/s11097-013-9305-3

Dennett, D. (1992). The Self as a Center of Narrative Gravity. In F. S. Kessel, P. M. Cole, D. L. Johnson & M. D. Hakel (Eds.), *Self and consciousness: Multiple perspectives* (pp. 103-115). New York, NY: Lawrence L. Erlbaum Associates, Inc.

du Sautoy, M. (2016). *The Great Unknown: Seven Journeys to the Frontiers of Science.* New York, NY: Viking. ISBN-13: 978-0735221802

Dunleavy, J., and Milton, P. (2010) "Student engagement for effective teaching and deep learning." *Education Canada,* November 2008, pp. 4-8. Canadian Education Association (cea-ace.ca)

Dupont, S., Galand, B., Nils, F., and Hospel, V. (2014) "Social Context, Self-Perceptions And Student Engagement: A Sem Investigation Of The Self-System Model Of Motivational Development (Ssmmd)." *Electronic Journal of Research in Educational Psychology 12*(1) 5-32. doi: 10.14204/ejrep.32.13081.

Early, D.M., Rogge, R.D., and Deci, E.L. (2014) "Engagement, Alignment, and Rigor as Vital Signs of High-Quality Instruction: A Classroom Visit Protocol for

Instructional Improvement and Research." *The High School Journal 97*(4) 219-39. doi: 10.1353/hsj.2014.0008.

Emdin, C. (2017). *For White Folks Who Teach in the Hood ... and the Rest of Yall Too: Reality Pedagogy and Urban Education*. Boston, MA: Beacon Press.

Farris-Berg, K., Dirkswager, E. J., & Junge, A. (2013). *Trusting Teachers with School Success: What Happens When Teachers Call the Shots*. Lanham, MD: Rowman & Littlefield Education.

Fertig, B. (2009). *Why cant u teach me 2 read? Three Students and a Mayor Put Our Schools to the Test*. New York, NY: Farrar, Straus and Giroux.

Friedman, R., Deci, E.L., Elliot, A.J., Moller, A.C., & Aarts, H. (2010). Motivational synchronicity: Priming motivational orientations with observations of others' behaviors. *Motivation and Emotion, 34*(1), 34-38. doi:10.1007/s11031-009-9151-3

Fullan, M., and Quinn, J.,. (2016) *Coherence: the right drivers in action for schools, districts, and systems*. Thousand Oaks, CA: Corwin.

Fullan, M., Quinn, J., & McEachen, J. (2018). *Deep Learning: Engage the World Change the World*. Thousand Oaks, CA: Corwin.

Gabor, A., (2018) *After the Education Wars: How Smart Schools Upend the Business of Reform*. New York, NY: The New Press. ISBN 978-1-62097-199-4

Gallup, Inc. (2010, August 12). *Student Poll: 34% in Grades 5-12 Hopeful, Engaged, Thriving*. Retrieved March 08, 2018, from http://news.gallup.com/poll/141854/student-poll-grades-hopeful-engaged-thriving.aspx

Gallup, Inc. (2011) *Gallup Student Poll- National Cohort Fall 2011—Lindbergh Elementary—Madison Metropolitan* (Rep.)

Gallup, Inc. (2012) *Gallup Student Poll—America's Promise Alliance 2012-2013 All Sites* (Rep.)

Gallup, Inc. (2013) *Gallup Student Poll Results: U.S. Overall Fall 2013* (Rep.).

Gallup, Inc. (2014) *Gallup Student Poll Results: U.S. Overall Fall 2014* (Rep.).

Gallup, Inc. (2015) *Gallup Student Poll Engaged Today — Ready for Tomorrow: U.S. Overall Fall 2015 Scorecard* (Rep.).

Gallup, Inc. (2016) *Gallup Student Poll Engaged Today — Ready for Tomorrow: U.S. Overall Fall 2016 Scorecard* (Rep.). Accessed May 29, 2017. http://www.gallupstudentpoll.com/197492/2016-national-scorecard.aspx.

Gallup, Inc. (2017a). *Gallup Student Poll Engaged Today — Ready for Tomorrow U.S. Overall Fall 2017 Scorecard* (Rep.). Accessed March 2, 2018. http://www.gallupstudentpoll.com/file/197492/GSP_US_Overall_2017_final.pdf.

Gallup Inc. (2017b). Gallup Student Poll Brochure. Retrieved March 8, 2018, from http://www.gallupstudentpoll.com/187751/gallup-student-poll-brochure.aspx

Gardner, H. (2004) *The unschooled mind: How children think and how schools should teach*. New York: Basic Books.

Gatto, J. T. (2005). *Dumbing Us Down*. Gabriola Island, BC: New Society.

Gilbert, D. T. (2006). *Stumbling on happiness*. New York, NY: A.A. Knopf.

Gottfried, A.E. (1985). Academic intrinsic motivation in elementary and junior high school students. *Journal of Educational Psychology, 77*(6), 631-645. doi: 10.1037/0022-0663.77.6.631

Gottfried, A.E., Fleming, J.S., & Gottfried, A.W. (2001). Continuity of academic intrinsic motivation from childhood through late adolescence: A longitudinal study. *Journal of Educational Psychology, 93*(1), 3-13. DOI: 10.1037/0022-0663.93.1.3

Greene, J.D. (2013) *Moral tribes: emotion, reason, and the gap between us and them.* New York: The Penguin Group.

Haidt, J. (May 18, 2007) "The new synthesis in moral psychology." *Science*, 998-1002. doi: 10.1126/science.1137651

Haidt, J. (2012) *The righteous mind: Why good people are divided by politics and religion.* New York, NY: Pantheon/ Random House.

Hanson, J., & Yosifon, D. (2003). The Situation: An Introduction to the Situational Character, Critical Realism, Power Economics, and Deep Capture. *University of Pennsylvania Law Review,*152(1), 129-346. doi: 10.2307/3313062

Hanson, J., and Yosifon, D. (2004) "The Situational Character: A Critical Realist Perspective on the Human Animal." *Georgetown Law Journal 93*(1) 1-179. from http://digitalcommons.law.scu.edu/facpubs/59

Hargreaves, A., & Fullan, M. (2012). *Professional Capital: Transforming Teaching in Every School.* New York, NY: Teachers College Press.

Harter, J. (2017, December 20). *Dismal employee engagement is a sign of global mismanagement.* Retrieved March 03, 2018, from http://news.gallup.com/opinion/gallup/224012/dismal-employee-engagement-sign-global-mismanagement.aspx

Harter, S. (1981). A new self-report scale of intrinsic versus extrinsic orientation in the classroom: Motivational and informational components. *Developmental Psychology, 17*(3), 300-312. doi: 10.1037/0012-1649.17.3.300

Harter, S., & Jackson, B.K. (1992). Trait vs. nontrait conceptualizations of intrinsic/extrinsic motivational orientation. *Motivation and Emotion, 16*(3), 209-230.

Hastings, M., and Agrawal, S. (January 9, 2015) "Lack of Teacher Engagement Linked to 2.3 Million Missed Workdays." Gallup.com. Accessed May 18, 2017. http://www.gallup.com/poll/180455/lack-teacher-engagement-linked-million-missed-workdays.aspx.

Headden, S., & McKay, S. (2015). Motivation Matters: How New Research Can Help Teachers Boost Student Engagement (Rep.). Retrieved February 24, 2018, from Carnegie Foundation for the Advancement of Teaching website: https://www.carnegiefoundation.org/resources/publications/motivation-matters-how-new-research-can-help-teachers-boost-student-engagement/

Heller, R., Wolfe, R. E., & Steinberg, A. (Eds.). (2017). *Rethinking Readiness: Deeper Learning for College, Work, and Life.* Cambridge, MA: Harvard Education Press.

Hodgins, H. ., Liebeskind, E., & Schwartz, W. (1996). Getting out of hot water: Facework in social predicaments. *Journal of Personality and Social Psychology, 71*(4), 300–314. doi: 10.1037//0022-3514.71.2.300

HSCA (Harvard-Smithsonian Center for Astrophysic)s, Science Education Department, Science Media Group. (1987). *A Private Universe.* Retrieved February 24, 2018, from https://www.learner.org/resources/series28.html ISBN: 1-57680-404-6

HSCA (Harvard-Smithsonian Center for Astrophysics), Science Education Department, Science Media Group. (1997). *Minds of Our Own*. Retrieved February 24, 2018, from https://www.learner.org/resources/series26.html ISBN: 1-57680-064-4

Hunter, J.P., & Csikszentmihalyi, M. (2003). The positive psychology of interested adolescents. *Journal of Youth and Adolescence, 32*(1) 27-35. DOI: 10.1023/A:1021028306392

Jang, H., Reeve, J., & Deci, E.L. (2010). Engaging students in learning activities: It is not autonomy support or structure but autonomy support and structure. *Journal of Educational Psychology, 102*(3), 588-600. doi: 10.1037/a0019682

Johnson, S. (2011). *Where good ideas come from: The seven patterns of innovation*. New York, NY: Riverhead Books.

Kahneman, D. (2011) *Thinking, fast and slow*. New York: Farrar, Straus and Giroux.

Kasser, T., & Ryan, R.M. (1993). A dark side of the American dream: Correlates of financial success as a central life aspiration. *Journal of Personality and Social Psychology, 65*(2), 410–422. doi: 10.1037//0022-3514.65.2.410.

Kenrick, D.T., Griskevicius, V., Neuberg, S.L., & Schaller, M. (2010). Renovating the pyramid of needs: Contemporary extensions built upon ancient foundations. *Perspectives on Psychological Science, 5*(3), 292–314. doi: 10.1177/1745691610369469.

Kim, A. (2015) *Personalized learning playbook: Why the time is now... and how to do it*. Washington, DC: Education Elements.

Klein, G. (1999). *Sources of power: How people make decisions*. Cambridge, MA: MIT Press.

Klein, G. (2011). *Streetlights and Shadows: Searching for the Keys to Adaptive Decision Making*. Cambridge, MA: MIT Press.

Koestner, R., Ryan, R. M., Bernieri, F., & Holt, K. (1984). Setting limits on children's behavior: The differential effects of controlling vs. informational styles on intrinsic motivation and creativity. *Journal of Personality, 52*(3), 233-248. http://dx.doi.org/10.1111/j.1467-6494.1984.tb00879.x

Kysilko, D., ed. (2014) The State Education Standard, March 2014. from http://www.nasbe.org/wp-content/uploads/Standard_Mar2014_full_online.pdf

Lakoff, G., and Johnson, M. (1999) *Philosophy in the flesh: The embodied mind & its challenge to western thought*. New York, NY: Basic Books.

Lepper, M. R., Corpus, J. H., & Iyengar, S. S. (2005). Intrinsic and extrinsic motivation orientations in the classroom: Age differences and academic correlates. *Journal of Educational Psychology, 97*(2), 184-196. doi: 10.1037/0022-0663.97.2.184

Littrell, R.F. (2012) Academic anterograde amnesia and what Maslow really said. Auckland, New Zealand: Centre for Cross Cultural Comparisons Working Paper CCCC 2012.3, http://crossculturalcentre.homestead.com/WorkingPapers.html.

Loehr, J., & Schwartz, T. (2003). *The Power of Full Engagement: Managing Energy, Not Time, Is the Key to High Performance and Personal Renewal*. New York, NY: Free Press.

Marks, H.M. (2000). Student Engagement in Instructional Activity: Patterns in the Elementary, Middle, and High School Years. *American Educational Research Journal, 37*(1), 153-184. doi: 10.2307/1163475

Martela, F., & Ryan, R. M. (2016). The Benefits of Benevolence: Basic Psychological Needs, Beneficence, and the Enhancement of Well-Being. *Journal of Personality, 84*(6), 750–764. doi: 10.1111/jopy.12215

Martela, F., Ryan, R.M. & Steger, M.F. (2017). Meaningfulness as satisfaction of autonomy, competence, relatedness, and beneficence: Comparing the four satisfactions and positive affect as predictors of meaning in life. *Journal of Happiness Studies.* Advance online publication. doi: 10.1007/s10902-017-9869-7

Martinez, M. R., & McGrath, D. (2014). *Deeper Learning How Eight Innovative Public Schools Are Transforming Education in the Twenty-First Century.* New York, NY: The New Press.

Meece, J.L., Blumenfeld, P.C., & Hoyle, R.H. (1988). Student' goal orientations and cognitive engagement in classroom activities. *Journal of Educational Psychology, 80*(4), 514-523. doi: 10.1037//0022-0663.80.4.514.

Mehta, J., and Fine, S. (2015) The Why, What, Where, and How of Deeper Learning in American Secondary Schools. (Rep.) Students at the Center: Deeper Learning Research Series. Boston, MA: Jobs for the Future. from http://studentsatthecenterhub.org/resource/the-why-what-where-and-how-of-deeper-learning-in-american-secondary-schools/

Mehta, J., and Fine, S. (2019) *In Search of Deeper Learning.* Cambridge. MA: Harvard University Press

Mehta, J. (2018, January 04). A Pernicious Myth: Basics Before Deeper Learning. Retrieved January 21, 2019, from http://blogs.edweek.org/edweek/learning_deeply/2018/01/a_pernicious_myth_basics_before_deeper_learning.html?cmp=soc-edit-tw

Miller, M.R., Latham, B., and Cahill, B. (2017) *Humanizing the education machine: how to create schools that turn disengaged kids into inspired learners.* Hoboken, NJ: John Wiley & Sons, Inc.

Moore, T. O. (2010, June 21). The Making of an Educational Conservative. Retrieved July 12, 2019, from https://www.claremont.org/crb/article/the-making-of-an-educational-conservative/

Musu-Gillette, L., Zhang, A., Wang, K., Zhang, J., Kemp, J., Diliberti, M., and Oudekerk, B.A. (2018). *Indicators of School Crime and Safety: 2017* (NCES 2018-036/NCJ 251413). National Center for Education Statistics, U.S. Department of Education, and Bureau of Justice Statistics, Office of Justice Programs, U.S. Department of Justice. Washington, DC.

NCES (National Center for Education Statistics). (2016) "Fast Facts: Dropout Rate." National Center for Education Statistics (NCES) Home Page, a part of the U.S. Department of Education. Accessed May 18, 2017. https://nces.ed.gov/fastfacts/display.asp?id=16.

Newell, R. J., & Van Ryzin, M. J. (2009). *Assessing what really matters in schools: creating hope for the future.* Lanham, MD: Rowman & Littlefield Education.

Nisbett, R. E. (2007). Eastern and Western Ways of Perceiving the World. In Shoda, Y., Cervone, D., & Downey, G. (Eds.). *Persons in context: building a science of the individual* (pp. 62-83). New York, NY: The Guilford Press.

Nishimura, T., and Suzuki, T. (2016) "Basic Psychological Need Satisfaction and Frustration in Japan: Controlling for the Big Five Personality Traits." *Japanese Psychological Research, 58*(4) 320-31. doi: 10.1111/jpr.12131.

Nord, C., Roey, S., Perkins, R., Lyons, M., Lemanski, N., Brown, J., and Schuknecht, J. (2011). The Nation's Report Card: America's High School Graduates (NCES

2011-462). U.S. Department of Education, National Center for Education Statistics. Washington, DC: U.S. Government Printing Office.

NPDL (New Pedagogies for Deep Learning). "Homepage – New Pedagogies for Deep Learning." Accessed April 30, 2017. http://npdl.global/.

Otis, N., Grouzet, F.M.E., & Pelletier, L.G. (2005). Latent motivational change in an academic setting: A 3-year longitudinal study. *Journal of Educational Psychology, 97*(2), 170-183. DOI: 10.1037/0022-0663.97.2.170

Peake, P. K. (2017). Delay of Gratification: Explorations of How and Why Children Wait and Its Linkages to Outcomes Over the Life Course. In J.R. Stevens (ed.), *Impulsivity, Nebraska Symposium on Motivation 64,* 7-60, Springer International Publishing AG. doi: 10.1007/978-3-319-51721-6_2

Pinker, S. (2002). *The blank slate: The modern denial of human nature.* New York, NY: Viking.

Pintrich, P.R. (2003). A motivational science perspective on the role of student motivation in learning and teaching contexts. *Journal of Educational Psychology, 95*(4), 667-686. doi: 10.1037/0022-0663.95.4.667

Pintrich, P.R., & Garcia, T. (1991). Student goal orientation and self-regulation in the college classroom. In M. L. Maehr and P. R. Pintrich (Eds.), *Advances in Motivation and Achievement* (pp. 371-402). Greenwich, CT: JAI Press.

Prawat, R.S., Grissom, S., & Parish, T. (1979). Affective development in children, grades 3 through 12. *The Journal of Genetic Psychology, 135*(1), 37-49. doi: 10.1080/00221325.1979.10533415

Radel, R., Sarrazin, P., Legrain, P., & Wild, T.C. (2010). Social contagion of motivation between teacher and student: analyzing underlying processes. *Journal of Educational Psychology, 102*(3), 577-587. doi: 10.1037/a0019051

Raymond, J. P. (2018). *Wildflowers: A School Superintendent's Challenge to America.* San Francisco, CA: SF Press.

Reeve, J. (2009). Why teachers adopt a controlling motivating style toward students and how they can become more autonomy supportive. *Educational Psychologist, 44*(3), 159-175. doi: 10.1080/00461520903028990

Reeve, J. (2013). How students create motivationally supportive learning environments for themselves: The concept of agentic engagement. *Journal of Educational Psychology,* 105(3), 579-595. doi: 10.1037/a0032690

Reis, H.T., Sheldon, K.M., Gable, S.L., Roscoe, J., & Ryan, R. (2000). Daily well-being: The role of autonomy, competence, and relatedness. *Personality & Social Psychology Bulletin, 22*(4), 419-435 . doi: 10.1177/0146167200266002

Robinson, K., and Aronica, L. (2016) *Creative schools.* New York, NY: Penguin Books.

Rose, T. (2016). *The End of Average: How we succeed in a world that values sameness.* New York, NY: HarperCollins.

Russell, N. J. (2011). Milgrams obedience to authority experiments: Origins and early evolution. *British Journal of Social Psychology, 50*(1), 140-162. doi: 10.1348/014466610x492205

Ryan, R.M., & Connell, J. P. (1989). Perceived locus of causality and internalization: Examining reasons for acting in two domains. *Journal of Personality and Social Psychology, 57*(5), 749–761. doi: 10.1037//0022-3514.57.5.749

Ryan, R.M., & Deci, E.L. (2000a). Self-determination theory and the facilitation of intrinsic motivation, social development, and well-being. *American Psychologist, 55*(1), 68-78. doi: 10.1037/0003-066X.55.1.68

Ryan, R.M. & Deci, E.L. (2000b). The darker and brighter sides of human existence: Basic psychological needs as a unifying concept. *Psychological Inquiry, 11*(4), 319–338.

Ryan, R.M., & Deci, E.L. (2006). Self-regulation and the problem of human autonomy: Does psychology need choice, self-determination, and will?. *Journal of Personality 74*(6), doi: 10.1111/j.1467-6494.2006.00420.x

Sansone, C., & Harackiewicz, J.M. (Eds.). (2000). *Intrinsic and extrinsic motivation: The search for optimal motivation and performance.* San Diego: Academic Press.

Sachse, P., Beermann, U., Martini, M., Maran, T., Domeier, M., & Furtner, M. R. (2017). "The world is upside down" – The Innsbruck Goggle Experiments of Theodor Erismann (1883–1961) and Ivo Kohler (1915–1985). *Cortex, 92,* 222-232. doi: 10.1016/j.cortex.2017.04.014

Sapolsky, R. M. (2017). *Behave: The Biology of Humans at Our Best and Worst.* New York, NY: Penguin Press.

Schüler, J., Brandstätter, V., and Sheldon, K.M. (2012) "Do implicit motives and basic psychological needs interact to predict well-being and flow? Testing a universal hypothesis and a matching hypothesis." *Motivation and Emotion 37*(3), 480-95. doi: 10.1007/s11031-012-9317-2.

Schulz, R., & Hanusa, B. H. (1978). Long-term effects of control and predictability-enhancing interventions: Findings and ethical issues. *Journal of Personality and Social Psychology. 36*(11), 1194-1201. doi: 10.1037//0022-3514.36.11.1194

Seligman, M. E. P. (2002). *Authentic Happiness : using the new positive psychology to realize your potential for lasting fulfillment.* Free Press.

Sheldon, K.M., Ryan, R., & Reis, H.T. (1996). What makes for a good day? Competence and autonomy in the day and in the person. *Personality and Social Psychology Bulletin, 22*(12), 1270-1279. doi: 10.1177/01461672962212007

Shoda, Y., Cervone, D., & Downey, G. (Eds.). (2007). *Persons in context: building a science of the individual.* New York, NY: Guilford.

Siegel, D. J. (2012). *The developing mind: toward a neurobiology of interpersonal experience.* New York, NY: Guilford Press.

Spitz, R.A. (1965). *The First Year of Life.* New York: International Universities Press.

Stipek, D. (2002). *Motivation to learn: Integrating theory and practice.* (4th ed.). Boston, MA: Allyn and Bacon.

Stone, S., Johnson, K.M., Beall, E., Meindl, P., Smith, B., and Graham, J. (2014) "Political psychology." *WIREs Cognitive Science.* doi: 10.1002/wcs.1293.

Taormina, R.J. & Gao, J.H. (2013) Maslow and the motivation hierarchy: Measuring satisfaction of the needs. *American Journal of Psychology 126*(2), 155-177. doi: 10.5406/amerjpsyc.126.2.0155.

Tay, L., & Diener, E. (2011). Needs and subjective well-being around the world. *Journal of Personality and Social Psychology. 101*(2):354-65. doi: 10.1037/a0023779

Taylor, I.M., Ntoumanis, N., & Standage, M. (2008). A self-determination theory approach to understanding the antecedents of teachers' motivational strategies in physical education. *Journal of Sport & Exercise Psychology, 30*(1), 75-94. doi: 10.1037/0022-0663.99.4.747

Thomas, K. W. (2000). *Intrinsic Motivation at Work: Building Energy & Commitment.* San Francisco, CA: Berrett-Koehler.

Toshalis, E. (2016). *Make Me! Understanding and Engaging Student Resistance in School* (2nd ed.). Cambridge, MA: Harvard Education Press.

Van Ryzin, M.J., A.A. Gravely, and C.J. Roseth. (2009) "Autonomy, Belongingness, and Engagement in School as Contributors to Adolescent Psychological Well-Being." *Journal of Youth and Adolescence. 38*(1), 1-12. doi: 10.1007/s10964-007-9257-4.

Van Ryzin, M.J. (2011) Protective Factors at School: Reciprocal Effects Among Adolescents' Perceptions of the School Environment, Engagement in Learning, and Hope. *Journal of Youth and Adolescence. 40*(12), 1568–1580. doi: 10.1007/s10964-011-9637-7.

Vedder-Weiss, D., & Fortus, D. (2011). Adolescents' declining motivation to learn science: Inevitable or not?. *Journal of Research in Science Teaching, 48*(2), 199-216. doi: 10.1002/tea.20398

Véronneau, M.H., Koestner, R.F., & Abela, J.R.Z. (2005). Intrinsic need satisfaction and wellbeing in children: An application of the self-determination theory. *Journal of Social and Clinical Psychology, 24*(2), 280-292. doi: 10.1521/jscp.24.2.280.62277.

Wahba, M.A., & Bridwell, L.G., (1976) Maslow reconsidered: A review of research on the need hierarchy theory. *Organizational Behavior and Human Performance. 15*(2), 212-240. doi:10.1016/0030-5073(76)90038-6.Baard, P.P., Deci, E.L., & Ryan, R.M. (2004). Intrinsic need satisfaction: A motivational basis of performance and well-being in two work settings. *Journal of Applied Social Psychology*, 34, 2045–2068. doi: 10.1111/j.1559- 1816.2004.tb02690.x

Walker, T. D. (2017). *Teach like Finland: 33 Simple Strategies for Joyful Classrooms.* New York, NY: W.W. Norton & Company.

Weiss, J. (2016, August 15). Back to basics through the years. Retrieved January 11, 2019, from https://www.chicagoreporter.com/back-basics-through-years/

Wigfield, A., Eccles, J.S., & Rodriguez, D. (1998). The development of children's motivation in school contexts. *Review Research in Education, 23*, 73-118. Retrieved 22 May, 2013 from: http://www.jstor.org/stable/1167288

Williamson, K. D. (2016, July 01). The Road to Rationalia. Retrieved February 24, 2018, from https://www.nationalreview.com/2016/06/neil-degrasse-tysons-rationality-pipe-dream/

Wolfe, R. E., Steinberg, A., & Hoffman, N. (Eds.). (2013). *Anytime, Anywhere: Student-Centered Learning for Schools and Teachers.* Cambridge, MA: Harvard Education Press.

Zhao, Y. (2009) *Catching up, or, Leading the way: American education in the age of globalization.* Alexandria, Va: Association for Supervision and Curriculum Development.

Zimbardo, P. (2013). *The lucifer effect: Understanding how good people turn evil.* New York: Random House.

ABOUT THE AUTHOR

Don Berg is the Executive Director of the non-profit Deeper Learning Advocates. He has over 20 years of experience leading children in self-directed educational settings, both in schools and in out-of-school programs. He is also the founder and CEO of Attitutor Services which provides consulting services to school leaders who want to build their organization's capacity to support deeper learning. He lives at the Joyful Llama Ranch near Portland, Oregon, USA.

56061277R00096

Made in the USA
Middletown, DE
22 July 2019